THE UNWRITTEN RULES OF THE HIGHLY EFFECTIVE JOB SEARCH

**The Proven Program Used by the
World's Leading Career Services Company**

Orville Pierson

McGRAW-HILL

New York | Chicago | San Francisco | Lisbon | London
Madrid | Mexico City | Milan | New Delhi | San Juan
Seoul | Singapore | Sydney | Toronto

The *McGraw·Hill* Companies

This publication is designed to provide accurate and authoritative information in regard to the subject matter covered. It is sold with the understanding that the publisher is not engaged in rendering legal, accounting, or other professional service. If legal advice or other expert assistance is required, the services of a competent professional person should be sought.—*From a Declaration of Principles Jointly Adopted by a Committee of the American Bar Association and a Committee of Publishers and Associations*

4 5 6 7 8 9 0   DOC/DOC   0 9

ISBN-13: 978-0-07-146404-8
ISBN-10: 0-07-146404-2

McGraw-Hill books are available at special discounts to use as premiums and sales promotions, or for use in corporate training programs. For more information, please write to the Director of Special Sales, Professional Publishing, McGraw-Hill, Two Penn Plaza, New York, NY 10121-2298. Or contact your local bookstore.

Library of Congress Cataloging-in-Publication Data

Pierson, Orville.
   The unwritten rules of the highly effective job search : the proven program used by the world's leading career services company / by Orville Pierson.
      p. cm.
   ISBN 0-07-146404-2 (alk. paper)
   1. Job hunting—United States. 2. Career changes—United States. 3. Self-presentation.
I. Title: How to find a job you love. II. Title.
   HF5382.75.U6P483 2006
   650.14'0973—dc22

                                        2005015994

Contents

Preface

1. Orville, Jessie, Ben, and The Pierson Method   **1**
In this chapter, I'll tell you why I wrote this book, and how it can help you find a good new job. I'll introduce you to Ben and Jessica Williams and to the Pierson Method, the proven job hunting system used by over 600,000 people to find good new jobs.

2. The Job Search Project   **13**
If you've tried everything in job search and it's not working very well, this chapter is for you. Most people in job search have a weak plan—or none at all. If you plan and organize your search project using the steps in this chapter, you're well on your way to success.

3. Why You Need Progress Measurements   **35**
Before you get a job offer—or even before your first interview—how do you know if you are making progress? Learn why you need to be able to answer that question and take a look at the most common pitfalls in search—and how to avoid them.

4. How Hiring Really Happens   **49**
Professional hunters plan the hunt based on their knowledge of how their quarry behave. In the same way, your job hunting activities need to be based on how hiring really happens, not on how it is supposed to happen or how people say it happens.

5. Your Project Plan   **73**
In job search, like other projects, you need to plan your work, then work your plan. Your Project Plan is based on your personal answers to three key questions. Armed with a Project Plan, you are ready to "work smart" in your search.

6. Choosing Your Next Job   **95**
The first step in your Project Plan is deciding what kind of work you want to look for, based on your longer term plans. Don't be afraid to "narrow your options," a bit: a clear focus is essential to success. Here's how to find the answer that's right for you.

7. Your Target List   121

Most people wouldn't consider starting a search without a resume. A Target List is just as important, but most people don't even consider having one. This chapter tells you how to create one and how to use it to speed your search.

8. Your Core Message   137

Potential employers—and others you talk to in a search—make decisions about you based largely on what comes out of your mouth. In a search, you will repeat a Core Message about yourself many times. Here's how to make it good.

9. How Many Fish Are in That Pond?   157

Job hunting with a poor Project Plan is like fishing in a pond with only two fish: Even if you are really good at fishing, you might not catch anything. Here's a Reality Check to make sure that using your Project Plan is like fishing in a well stocked pond.

10. The Seven Search Techniques   175

The good news about job search is that there are only seven search techniques and none of them are complicated. You do not need to use all seven, but you must use some of them. Here's what they are, and the pros and cons of using each.

11. Keeping Score   203

Here are some simple ways of keeping score in your search. If you're winning, keep on playing the same way. If not, make some changes. Your weekly score also tells you when you've done a good week's work. If you can do that by Thursday, take a long weekend.

12. The Pierson Method   225

This is a compact roadmap for success in search—a step-by-step summary of the Pierson Method and the most important points in this book. After you read the book, you may want to use this chapter to review the entire system as you conduct your search.

Special Section: Team Up for a Successful Search   241

Like many activities, job hunting can be easier when you do it as part of a team. If you'd prefer not to do your search alone or if you'd like to start a team for others who are job hunting, this chapter is for you.

Additional Resources   269

Acknowledgments   279

The Man Who Prayed to Win the Lottery

Once there was a man named Sam who wanted to win the lottery. He knew that the odds were not so good. But he was a religious man and also knew that with God all things are possible.

So he prayed every morning that he would win the lottery. But he didn't win.

So he began praying three times a day to win the lottery. He continued this for over a year, but he still didn't win.

Finally, he began praying constantly, all day every day, to win the lottery. He did this for several years. He still didn't win, but his faith did not fail. He continued to pray, "Lord, it's me, Sam. Please let me win the lottery."

One day, God actually responded. "Sam," the Lord said, "it would help if you would buy a ticket."

The odds of your finding a great new job are thousands of times better than the odds of winning the lottery. But in both cases, you need to make some intelligent effort.

I have heard it said that self effort and God's grace are like the two wings of a bird—which together enable us to soar through life, as well as a job search. Whether you would prefer to call it "God's grace" or "the Power of the Universe" or just plain "good luck," the other half of the equation is definitely the systematic, well organized self effort that is the topic of this book.

Finding a job usually takes much more effort than buying a lottery ticket. But most people don't know how much effort is needed, what *kind* of efforts are the most effective or where to turn to get good advice. To help you with these and all the challenges of job hunting, I have boiled it down to the essentials, twelve steps that people call the Pierson Method. I'll be your guide throughout the book, explaining the steps as we go.

The two characters in my journal entries, Ben and Jessie Williams, are completely fictional, but represent the thoughts and reactions of the thousands of real people I have worked with in job search.

I hope you enjoy the book. More importantly, I hope it will help you find the work you need and want. And I hope you'll thrive in that work for a good long time.

Orville Pierson
January 2006

About the Author

Orville Pierson is Senior Vice President, Corporate Director of Program Design and Service Delivery for Lee Hecht Harrison (LHH), the leading global career services company with 200 offices worldwide.

He is the principal or sole author of dozens of LHH career publications, Web sites, and videos, and has trained hundreds of career consultants in the United States and the United Kingdom in the use of LHH's leading edge job search and career programs. Over the years, his career books have been provided to over 1,000,000 private clients of career services firms. However, this book marks the first time that Orville's unique job search system, the Pierson Method, has been made available to the general public.

Yale-educated, Orville has been in the career services field since 1977, as a program and process designer, author, career coach, speaker, facilitator, and consultant.

I'm Orville Pierson. I'm a job search expert.

Over the years, I devised the Pierson method as a way to teach my friends and relatives how to find better jobs faster.

They said I should put it in a book so everyone could use it.

Here it is.

CHAPTER ONE

Orville, Jessie, Ben, and the Pierson Method

My name is Orville Pierson. People who hear my name before they meet me often imagine that I'll turn out to be smart. Or nerdy, like that Orville who wears a bow tie and horn-rimmed glasses while he sells popcorn. Some people think of Orville and Wilbur Wright, but so far, no one has expected me to be a pilot.

Actually, I'm not a popcorn man or a pilot. I'm an expert in careers and job hunting. I've spent most of my adult life coaching people on finding jobs and teaching professional career consultants how to do the same.

For the last 14 years I have been the Senior Vice President and Corporate Director of Program Design and Service Delivery for the leading global career services company. The title is so long that it barely fits on my business card, but it's a great job and I love it.

Some people see the title and think I'm a business executive, but I've never seen myself that way. I've always seen myself more as a teacher. And I guess you could say that I'm a guide. I guide people through the job search jungle to better jobs and better careers.

When I first started in this field in the 1970s, I began by working with individuals one at a time to coach and counsel them on their careers and how to find good new jobs. I worked with factory workers, business executives, and everyone in between. Most of my clients were unemployed, so it was important to them to get back to work as quickly as possible. By doing this, I learned a lot about what people need to do—and not do—to find jobs more quickly.

After I'd worked individually with hundreds of people for many years, I started teaching classes on how to find a job. I saw thousands of people in groups of 15 or 20. Again, I did this for many years.

HELPING 100,000 PEOPLE A YEAR FIND NEW JOBS

Now I work for Lee Hecht Harrison (LHH), which has over 200 locations around the world where people come for help with their careers. We have hundreds of career consultants helping up to 100,000 people a year find new jobs. My job is to create career books, training programs, and coaching services for our unemployed clients and to teach our career consultants, who are already very good, how to be even better at what they do.

Lee Hecht Harrison works mostly with people caught in those big downsizings you read about in the newspaper. Most of the country's largest and best employers provide career services for people they lay off. The unemployed people do not pay for the services. Their former employers pay the bill. Which is a good thing, since services can cost $5,000 to $10,000 per person, and even more for red carpet programs for executives.

I wasn't always a job search expert. When I was in kindergarten, I wanted to be a cowboy or a firefighter, not a career consultant. Later, I wanted to be a doctor. I actually did become a sculptor, a New York City cab driver, a clerk in a health food store, a carpenter, a construction site manager, an attendant in a mental hospital, and a group therapy leader—among other things.

Then one day I found myself newly married to a woman I loved dearly (and still do). She was nine months pregnant with the child we had both prayed for, and I was unemployed. We had a house, but not enough money to make the next mortgage payment. That's when I found my first job as a career consultant, which was interesting because I had never done career work before.

But some of my past experience was helpful and—much to my surprise—the fact that I had worked in a lot of different jobs suddenly became a plus. For someone with no prior experience in the job, I did very well at the start. In two or three years, I was well established in my new profession.

I liked career and job search assistance work from the very beginning and haven't gotten tired of it in 30 years. I've always felt that it was more like a calling than just a job. I love seeing unemployed people getting reemployed and seeing employed people make moves that make them happier in their work. Job search assistance is my hobby as well as my job. I sometimes volunteer to teach job hunting classes. And, of course, since people know what I do, they often ask me to help them find jobs.

WHAT I TELL MY FRIENDS AND RELATIVES ABOUT FINDING JOBS

When I'm volunteering to help people, I usually can't spend the time with them that Lee Hecht Harrison spends with a $10,000 client. So over the years, I've boiled everything I know down to a shorter version—including only the essentials, the things that people most need to know and most need to do (and not do) to find a good job. And I made a system out of it, a method. That's what I've put in the book you are holding: the condensed version, what I tell my friends and relatives, the Pierson Method.

In this book, I'll guide you all the way through your job search. I'll teach you to use the Pierson Method to be your own career consultant. I'll tell you how it all works, so you can write or improve your own resumé and answer many of your own questions. You may still need to use a book on resumé writing or salary negotiations, and if you do, come to my Web site, highlyeffectivejobsearch.com, and I'll suggest some. You won't get everything you would from having your own professional career consultant. But you won't get a bill for $10,000 either.

In the following chapters, I have explained the entire Pierson Method for you: what you need to do to find a great new job, and how you will know if you are on the right track. I expect you to learn some things from reading this book. But I also expect that you already know some of it and won't be surprised by what you read. After all, like most proven methods, this one includes a lot of good old common sense.

When they see what the Pierson Method is, some people are very relieved that they finally have a system to use in job hunting. If you like a more systematic approach than most job search books provide, you'll like the Pierson Method.

On the other hand, some people feel a little overwhelmed by such a complete system. If you're one of those people, don't worry. You don't have to do everything in this book to get a great new job. Many people use only parts of the Pierson Method and still succeed very nicely. So add some pieces of the method to whatever you're already doing. Or plan on doing 51 percent of the Pierson Method. Always remember: you only need one good job offer to succeed in search.

Just one.

All of the Important Points Are in a Large Font, Like This

To save you time and effort, I put the main points in this book in a large font. If you know exactly what I'm talking about in that big headline, you can probably skip the paragraphs after it and move on to the next big headline. I also summarized the entire Pierson Method in Chapter 12, so you can easily review it if you want to.

Since I know quite a lot about finding jobs, you might think that I have always found them easily. The truth is, like many people, I don't enjoy looking for a new job. Sometimes I've moved easily from one job to the next. Other times, like when I was first married, it was a struggle to find something.

I really didn't know what to do at all then. There was no Internet. With a baby on the way, I needed a better, career-track job. Most of the better jobs in the paper asked for experience I didn't have. I asked a friend of mine for advice. He knew an executive recruiter. After staring at the telephone for an hour or so, I called the recruiter, who actually returned my phone call!

I thought I had it all solved, until the recruiter asked me what kind of work I was looking for. I stumbled around, saying some things about helping people and communications. The recruiter was polite, but the call ended soon after that. Later, I learned that he handled only $50,000-a-year jobs in manufacturing management. I was looking for $10,000 or $12,000 a year (this was the 1970s, remember), and was very happy when I found something at the enormous salary of $15,000.

Even after I became a career consultant, I never liked looking for a new job, though I did it a couple of times. The telephone always seems to weigh 200 pounds. Very hard to pick up. Although I knew exactly what I needed to do and exactly how to do it, I never found it fun. It's that way for many people, at least in some parts of the search. I guess if most people liked the job search, I would have to look for a new and different career. There wouldn't be any career consultants.

One more thing. I use the words "job hunting" in this book, but I actually don't see job search as hunting. While there are some similarities between going hunting in the woods and looking for a new job, there are also some big differences. Both are good ways to put food on the table. In both, you need to understand your quarry and track some things down. But in job search, you won't need to kill anything—or anybody—though you may sometimes feel like it. And, in the end, I certainly hope that you'll like your new job or career so much you'll want to keep it alive and healthy for a good long time.

The other thing is that in job search, the animals to watch out for aren't out there in the woods. They're inside you. In your mind. The biggest obstacles to success are the inner beasts: fear, feeling worthless, lack of confidence, and many others. It's probably a good idea not to try to kill them, since they're likely to fight back. But you certainly need to keep your eye on them and proceed with courage, even though there is sometimes a beast behind every tree. More on that later.

THERE'S A JOB OUT THERE FOR EVERYONE—BUT YOU'VE GOT TO WORK TO FIND IT

Even though there are some difficulties and challenges, there is a job out there for you. My belief—and my experience—is that there is a job for everyone who needs one, in good times and bad.

Even when the unemployment rate is as high as 10 percent, most of the people who want jobs (90 percent of them, to be exact) are employed. You can see it as two rooms: a big gymnasium where the 90 percent are working, and a smaller room where the 10 percent stay. People are leaving the big room all the time. They quit, retire, die, leave the job market, or lose their jobs and get sent to the small room.

People from the small room are constantly moving to the big one to replace those who are leaving. The job market is not frozen—it's in constant motion. Who gets those jobs as they open up? The best qualified? Sometimes. The ones who are sitting in the small room waiting and hoping someone will come and get them? Not likely.

The people who consistently find jobs are the ones who get to work on a well-planned job search and don't quit. They keep working on it, even when it doesn't look good. If they are smart about what they do, they'll make the move faster. But even if they're not very good at job search, they'll still find a job if only they keep trying.

At least, that's how it all looks to me.

BEN AND JESSICA WILLIAMS

Before we close this chapter and get to work for real on your new job, I want to introduce you to my neighbors, Jessica Williams and her husband Ben. As it happened, Jessie lost her job when I was writing this book. I didn't hear about it immediately.

Just as I finished editing my final draft of this very page, my phone rang. It was Ben. Jessie, he said, had been unemployed for three months, looking for a new job, and having no luck at all.

I was surprised to hear she'd been out so long, because people I know usually talk to me about their careers and job searches. But Jessie, Ben said, had been wanting to "do it herself," an idea he obviously had never agreed with. I didn't agree with it either.

Ben went on to say that the two of them had been arguing about her job search—and practically everything else—for weeks. I wasn't surprised, because when someone is unemployed, the family stress level always rises. The other reason I wasn't surprised was because it was summer, the windows were open, and I had heard some bits and pieces of it.

But now, Ben said, Jessie had changed her mind. She wanted help. But she was so discouraged that she wouldn't call me herself. Would I talk to her? he wanted to know. I immediately agreed to do that. I've seen people discouraged about job search more times than I like to remember. I like helping them get their job searches working.

I recorded my conversation with her in my author's journal for you to read. As you'll see, Jessie and Ben both ended up discussing this book with me, chapter by chapter. With their permission, I have included samples of those conversations at the end of each chapter. They provide a couple of different perspectives and you may find them useful.

ORVILLE'S JOURNAL

JESSIE AND I DISCUSS HER JOB SEARCH, AND SHE IS THE FIRST TO USE THE PIERSON METHOD BOOK

"Ben said I had to come over and talk to you," is how Jessie started the conversation. She didn't look happy, sitting alone in the center of my living room couch.

"I'm glad you did," I said. "I'm happy to talk to you. Ben told me you're looking for a new job. Helping people find jobs is what I do."

"And did Ben tell you that I've completely messed up my job search? And that no one wants to hire me? I'll probably never get a job. I'll probably end up being a bag lady." Jessie had a flair for the dramatic.

"No, Ben didn't say any of that," I replied, "and I wouldn't have believed it anyway. You've always had a great career. So now they shut the place down and let everyone go. That's not your fault."

"Yeah, but it's my fault that I haven't found anything. It's been three months now. I haven't had a single job offer. Nothing. Nada. Zip. I don't know why I came over. I shouldn't be bothering you with this. You're not a magician. You can't fix it."

"You're right that I can't fix it," I replied, "but I might be able to tell *you* how to fix it. Do you want to try a different approach?"

"A different approach? Like what? Calling a thousand people and begging for a job? Standing on a street corner with a sign that says, 'Desperate. Will work for food'?"

"No," I said, "I was thinking of something less dramatic. Like planning your job search. What kind of work you want to do. Which organizations hire people like you. How you're going to talk to them. What you're going to say. Then you use the search techniques that work best for you. And measure your progress."

"It sounds complicated," Jessie said. "It sounds like a lot of work. And then I'll still be unemployed."

"Has your search been working?" I asked, as gently as I could. I knew the answer, but I needed to make the point, "Are you getting a lot of interviews?"

"No."

"Then maybe it's time to try a more systematic approach. I know it works. Over 600,000 people have used it to find new jobs. I'm writing a book on it right now. I was just doing a final edit on Chapter 1. You want to read it?"

"Sure," she said. "Why not? What have I got to lose? Besides, Ben says you're a big expert. Maybe it'll work. Is it hard?"

I shook my head. "No. It's not complicated. If it were, all of those people wouldn't have used it over the last 10 or 12 years.

"You may not need to do everything the book says," I added. "If you find a job before you do any of it—or even before you finish reading the book, that will be okay with me."

Jessie actually smiled a little. "Okay," she said, "I'll try it. You're right about one thing. What I'm doing now isn't working. Besides, I'm unemployed. I've got nothing better to do."

So Jessica Williams became the first person to use the Pierson Method book. I gave her the first few chapters, even though I hadn't finished editing all of them. I promised to give her the rest as soon as I printed them out.

Jessie and I agreed to discuss each chapter as she read it—
one every few days. Ben said he'd like to join in too, even
though he wasn't looking for a job. Jessie seemed a little reluc-
tant about having Ben in the conversations—probably because
they'd been arguing about her job search so much—but she
agreed.

FACT:	Job search is a work project.

Like any project, job search succeeds because you . . .

Get Ready:
Plan and prepare.

Get Moving:
Take a systematic approach.

Manage Your Search:
Use progress measurements.

CHAPTER TWO

The Job Search Project

The other day my daughter Sarah called to ask me if I'd fix a broken kitchen drawer in her condo. Sarah had just bought the place. She had hired a teenager, John, to help her clean it before she moved in. And she needed a minor repair in the kitchen. As a former carpenter and longtime handyman in my own house, I enjoy a good broken drawer now and then, so I agreed.

When I got to Sarah's new place, Sarah and John were already hard at work. John was one of the strongest, most energetic young men I'd ever seen. He was scrubbing the dirty back corners of the kitchen floor while Sarah finished up on the stove. Sarah had an array of cleaning supplies lined up on the kitchen counter, including, I noticed, three identical squeegees.

They paused to say good morning, then moved on to the living room and left me with the kitchen drawer. It turned out to be a bigger problem than I thought, and I had to make two trips to the hardware store. Later in the morning, when the drawer was fixed, I found out what the third squeegee was for. I helped the two of them clean the windows and we finished the whole job in time for Sarah to change clothes and get to her one o'clock appointment on time.

She later told me that she had stopped by the condo the night before and made a list of what she wanted to do and the supplies she'd need. She had intentionally worked in the same room with John all morning so she could make sure he knew what to clean and how to clean it. He was a great worker, but had very little housecleaning experience.

The whole thing reminded me of job search. Some job hunters are as well organized as Sarah. They plan it out, then work in an organized way, paying the most attention to the most important tasks. But many job hunters don't have enough experience in search to make a good plan. Then, if they also don't have an experienced guide, they might not do things as well as they could.

You really can't blame job hunters for getting lost in the search sometimes. Many of the books on job search don't offer any good way of organizing the job search project. And some career consultants are just as weak on the subject.

Including me, for the first 15 years of my career. During those years, I never examined how job search was taught. Finally, I figured out that the usual ways of teaching people job search were flawed. Most of the books and courses teach only search skills and techniques: resumé writing, interviewing, salary negotiation, determining career direction, networking, using recruiters, browsing the Internet, and the like.

Which is like teaching a housecleaner to use a mop or a squeegee—it's a good idea, but you also need some planning. While skills and techniques are important, they're only one part of what you need for an effective job search.

Over the years, I noticed that people had a tendency to wander in their search. They used the techniques, but weren't sure which ones to use or when to use them. Their efforts were disorganized, unfocused, unrealistic, and not particularly productive.

When I began working with people on a systematic project management approach to job search, everything changed. They learned to create a Project Plan and the project became focused, more like Sarah's cleaning project. As my career consultant colleagues and I developed progress measurements, our clients became very productive. They found work they liked. And they found it more quickly.

After nearly 30 years of working with people in search, I believe that planning and organizing a systematic search is essential. You may still need to learn some of the search techniques. But the keys to success are the steps I call the Pierson Method. It's based on measuring progress and managing the search project. I'll introduce you to it right here: It includes 12 steps in three phases: Get Ready, Get Moving, and Manage Your Search.

Underneath the steps, the Pierson Method is plain common sense. You start by seeing job search as a project, then you plan and manage it just as you do other work projects, large and small. Most people looking for a new job don't see what they are doing as work, much less as an organized project.

I've seen a lot of unemployed people who are in a life crisis because of their unemployment. And there's no doubt that it can be a genuine crisis, especially when it begins with an unexpected layoff. But then they treat their search as part of the crisis rather than as a work project. What you do with a crisis is cope with it, weather it. What you need to do with a work project is plan it and organize it. Here's how.

Job Search Is a Work Project

You get the best results when you:

Get ready: Plan and prepare.

Get moving: Take a systematic approach.

Manage your search: Use progress measurements.

Managing the job search project is not so different from managing other projects. If you are over the age of 18, I know that you have project management experience—in school, at home, or at work. If you're a 55-year-old manager, you may have managed large projects, with a big budget and lots of people reporting to you. Everyone has project management experience at home. Cleaning your house is a work project. Or throwing a party. Or fixing a leaky kitchen sink.

THE PIERSON METHOD OF JOB SEARCH

Get Ready			PLAN AND PREPARE
1. Read this book	**2.** Create a Project Plan	**3.** Do a Reality Check	**4.** Write your resumé

Get Moving			TAKE A SYSTEMATIC APPROACH
5. Gather information	**6.** Talk to people	**7.** Follow up	**8.** Test the Seven Search Techniques

Manage Your Search			USE PROGRESS MEASUREMENTS
9. Track your progress	**10.** Recheck your Project Plan	**11.** Interview	**12.** Start your new job

Managing a project is easier if you do that kind of work often. If you have thrown parties before, you can probably plan one in your head. But you might still put some things on paper: a shopping list or invitation list, for instance. If the party is a wedding reception, you will probably put much more on paper.

While you may have more experience with job search than with weddings, expert advice in planning and preparation can still save you time and trouble—as well as increasing your chances of finding a really good job. In this book, I'll take you through it, step by step, and show you how well-trained professional career consultants help people plan and prepare for search.

For people in job search, progress measurements are usually the most difficult part of managing the project. If you're doing a project you have done many times before, it's easy to gauge your progress. But most people don't have enough experience to do that in search. And most job search books don't include the topic at all. It's an essential part of the Pierson Method. We'll introduce it right here in Chapter 2, and you'll find more in Chapters 3 and 11.

Work projects have many elements in common. Multimillion-dollar construction projects, cleaning apartments, throwing parties, fixing kitchen sinks, and finding jobs all succeed more rapidly because of good planning, careful preparation, and progress measurements that tell you how you are doing. The Pierson Method covers all of these.

PROJECT PLANNING AND PREPARATION

If you are not a plumber, you probably don't fix leaky sinks very often. So if you decided to fix your own, you would be smart to start by talking to an expert—maybe that uncle of yours who is a plumber. While you might not need a plan on paper, you would certainly have one in your head. And you might have a couple of lists on paper. Your plan would tell you how to prepare, what parts to buy, and which tools to borrow. Then you could get it done without extra trips to the hardware store or two inches of water on the floor.

Project planning begins with knowing exactly what you want to get done. In fixing the kitchen sink, what you want is simple—no more puddles on the floor. In search, you might say, "That's also simple. I need a job." Or "I need a better job." But what *kind* of job would be best?

After you have defined the goal of your project, you are ready to plan and prepare. For a construction project, planning is a big job. After the architectural plan, there is planning for materials, labor, costs, the order in which things are done, and much more. Then there's preparation, including buying materials, getting a permit, hiring a work crew, and the like.

Job search is less complicated. Let's look at the essentials of planning and preparing for a search.

Plan and Prepare
It's not just a resumé.
Use a Project Plan.

In the Pierson Method, the first phase is "Get Ready: Plan and Prepare." This includes four steps: reading this book to learn how to conduct a systematic search, creating a Project Plan, doing a Reality Check on the Project Plan, and, finally, writing a resumé.

People often think that writing a resumé is the first thing to do in a job search. But if you have 30 years of experience—or even just three years—you could write a book about it. In a resumé, you'll only have a page or two. How will you decide what to say and what to leave out? You'll certainly want to mention the jobs you've had. Most of them, at least. But exactly what will you say about them? What will you emphasize?

Any one person could have six or eight different resumés, all of them honest representations of past experience. Sometimes those resumés would look so different that if you took the name off, it would be hard to tell they were all the same person.

The truth is, you'll have a much better resumé if you think about your Project Plan first. A good resumé talks about your ability to do a certain

group of jobs, not all jobs. That group is defined by your Professional Objective—your statement of what kind of work you want to do.

A good resumé also talks to a certain group of people, not to everyone. The Decision Makers in your chosen Target Market are the most important audience you need to reach. They are the people who could be your next boss. They are the people you need to convince. The resumé shows them why you're a good candidate for the kind of jobs that they fill. It speaks to them in their language about what's important to them.

A resumé that tries to convince everyone that you can do anything ends up not working well anywhere. In resumé writing and throughout your search, focus is the key to success. Your Project Plan provides that focus.

YOUR PROJECT PLAN AND REALITY CHECK

An effective Project Plan has three parts: your Professional Objective, your Target Market (which becomes your Target List), and your Core Message.

The first part, your Professional Objective, defines the kind of work you want—the next step in your career and the goal of your project. It is usually a group of similar and related jobs.

Defining your Professional Objective is important because your next job needs to fit your skills. If it doesn't, you'll have trouble doing it, as well as finding it. It would be good if it relied on those skills you enjoy using. It would be great if it were a job you liked so much that you were happy to go there on Monday mornings.

Exactly what kind of work would that be? And where would it be? In what kind of organization? The same job title can be a very different job in two different organizations. If you don't know exactly what you are looking for, planning a project to find it is difficult. The more precisely you can define your Professional Objective— what kind of job you want—the more focused your search project becomes.

Next, you will define your Target Market by figuring out which employers are most likely to hire people in that kind of job. While doing this, you are also deciding which kinds of employers you like, since working in a *place* you like is just as important as working in a *job* you like. Your Target Market is your personal job market and the focus of your search.

Once you've defined that group of employers, it's not difficult to create a Target List of your favorite organizations in that group. The Decision Makers in the right departments in the organizations on your Target List are the most important people you will talk to, not just in your resumé, but also in interviewing.

Get Ready			PLAN AND PREPARE
1. Read this book	**2.** Create a Project Plan	**3.** Do a Reality Check	**4.** Write your resumé
Learn the the Pierson Method.	Your Project Plan has three parts.	Make sure your personal job market is big enough.	Your resumé is based on your Core Message.

Professional Objective:	**Target Market:**	**Core Message:**
What kind of work you want to do.	What kind of organization you want to work for. This becomes a Target List.	How you will tell people you can do the work in your Professional Objective.

That's where your Core Message comes in. What you say in your resumé and what you say at an interview should be very similar. After all, you're doing the same thing in both places: convincing people that you can do a particular kind of work. And your search will work better if you tell everyone else you meet along the way the same thing. Some of them will tell others, and this will help you. So why not think about what Core Message you want to communicate as part of your initial planning?

Putting it all together, your Core Message describes how well you can do the work defined by your Professional Objective. Your Core Message is what you will say about yourself and your Professional Objective to your Target Market, those organizations on your Target List—in your resumé, in interviews, and in general conversations.

Once you have created this three-part Project Plan, you'll need to check it to make sure it's reasonable and workable. Chapter 9 explains a Reality Check based on information about your particular job market. Once your plan checks out, you move to preparation.

PREPARE A RESUMÉ; PREPARE FOR INTERVIEWING

If your project was fixing that leaky kitchen sink, your preparation might include getting out the tools and changing your clothes. It might include buying parts or borrowing a tool.

In your search project, preparation includes actually writing a resumé based on your Core Message. That resumé speaks to your chosen Target Market about you, building a case for your candidacy. It tells Decision Makers in your Target Market that you can do the jobs defined by your Professional Objective. Your resumé will be more powerful because you outlined your Project Plan—including your Core Message—before writing it.

Later, you'll do interview preparation works the same way: You'll prepare a message that will convince your particular group of Decision Makers—the people who hire for the jobs you want —that you can do the jobs suggested by your Professional Objective.

PREPARE A TARGET LIST

Defining your Target Market helps you write a strong resumé. It also helps you manage your search. After defining your Target Market, you can use that definition to create an actual list of targeted employers with names, addresses, and phone numbers. This Target List is an extremely useful tool in job search—every bit as important as a resumé. It not only focuses your communication, it focuses your actual work in search. Because you concentrate your efforts on employers you like, you're more likely to end up at one you like.

And, no, I'm not going to tell you to phone everyone on that Target List or send your resumé to all of them. While you might decide to do one of those, I'm going to suggest a better way to get your search moving, using your Target List as a vehicle to focus on the best employers for you and systematically pursuing them. We'll discuss how you can actually increase your odds of finding a great new job by making yourself known to Decision Makers *before* they have an opening. But now let's take a look at phase two.

Take a Systematic Approach

It's not just about the Internet, ads, and recruiters.
Talking to insiders before there is an opening
moves your search faster.

When you finish your planning and preparation, you are ready to begin work on the search project itself. What you'll see in phase two of the Pierson Method is how to "Get Moving" in your search in four steps. You'll start by gathering information. Then you'll informally talk to people and follow up with them, especially Decision Makers. And you'll use some of the Seven Search Techniques.

In the first of those four steps, you'll gather information on the employers on your Target List. You'll do this by going to the library, using the Internet, and talking to people who have information, or "asking around." You'll use the information you collect to decide which employers are the ones you want to concentrate on. You'll eliminate the ones you don't like and put more energy into pursuing the ones you do like.

TALK TO PEOPLE: INSIDERS AND DECISION MAKERS

In the second step, you'll learn how to get in touch with insiders at your targeted employers. It's not complicated and you don't need to have important contacts to do it. If you ask the right questions, you'll probably find that you already know some insiders or some people who can introduce you to them. These insiders are people at your own level. They are an important information source. They are also an easy way to get in touch with the Decision Maker who will be your boss in your new job.

You will very likely talk to the Decision Maker *before* they have an opening in order to get an inside track when the opening occurs. As you'll see in Chapter 4, over half of those who find new jobs do it that way, talking to the boss before there is an opening. You can too.

This isn't usually an interview—it's an informal conversation on the phone or in person, maybe lasting only a few minutes. It lets your next boss know that you exist, before they need someone. Later, when they do need someone, you're on the short list. Sometimes it happens by accident. But the Pierson Method is about doing it systematically and intentionally.

FOLLOW UP WITH DECISION MAKERS

The third step, following up with these Decision Makers after you've met them, is often neglected in job search. People who do it find jobs faster than those who don't. What happens here is letting a number of Decision Makers know of your availability and qualifications. Typically, they have no opening when they first hear of you. But you continue talking to Decision Makers, and the more of them you talk to, the more likely it is that one will have an opening tomorrow. If you've been following up with them, you're probably still on the short list—and possibly the only person on it.

The fourth and last step in getting your search moving is to use some of those Seven Search Techniques. It's important to pick the techniques most likely to work for you and not waste time on those that probably won't work in your situation. Chapter 10 will show you how to choose among them.

Get Moving			TAKE A SYSTEMATIC APPROACH
5. Gather information	6. Talk to people	7. Follow up	8. Test the Seven Search Techniques
Find out about employers on your Target List.	Talk to friends, insiders, and Decision Makers, but *not* about job openings.	You want Decision Makers to remember you.	Try them out: Ads, postings, staffing firms, and all the rest.

Manage Your Search
It's not just managing interviews.
**Use progress measurements and
recheck your Project Plan regularly.**

The third phase of the Pierson Method is "Manage Your Search: Use Progress Measurements." There are four steps in this phase: Track your progress (which I'll talk about a great deal), recheck your project plan, interview, and start your new job.

I'll tell you right now two of the most important things I've learned about job hunting. The first is that pretty much everyone who really wants to work finds a job. The second is that progress measurements are essential to keeping a search moving and managing it effectively.

The question is not, "Will I find a job?" If you want to find a job badly enough to be persistent in your search, you will find one. The real questions are how long it will take and how good the job will be.

The biggest reason that it takes some people much longer than necessary to find work is simple: They get discouraged and slow their efforts—or stop altogether. This is where progress measurements come in. Even if you're having a bad week and are feeling discouraged, progress measurements let you know if you're getting the job of job search done. If you are, you'll get there in a reasonable time.

The average person in the average job search talks to 25 different Decision Makers before getting hired by one of them. In order to find and get in touch with one of these Decision Makers, the average person talks to about 15 other people, mostly friends and acquaintances, with a couple of insiders thrown in.

It's not complicated. You talk to about a dozen friends and acquaintances, show them your Target List, and ask questions about the list. You are *not* looking for job openings in these conversations. It's too soon for that. You're looking for information about those organizations and the chance to meet an insider, someone like you who works where you want to work.

When you've met a few insiders, one of them introduces you to the Decision Maker, their boss, and maybe your next boss. You follow up with those Decision Makers. Later, after you've met a number of them, one of these Decision Makers has an opening and you're invited in for a formal interview.

All of this isn't something I made up. It's the way it really happens most of the time. There are some other ways, but this is how most people find new jobs. Sociologists have studied it repeatedly. They always say the same thing: People find jobs by "informally" talking to other people. If you have a Project Plan and get organized about those informal contacts, you can make it happen faster.

Progress measurements are the best way to get organized about informal contacts and everything else in your search. Because they're numerical, they keep you objective about what you're doing. You may have used some kind of numerical measurements in other projects, training for a race, for example.

If the project is one that you have a lot of experience with, measuring your progress is easy. For example, construction project managers

Manage Your Search		USE PROGRESS MEASUREMENTS	
9. Track your progress	10. Recheck your Project Plan	11. Interview	12. Start your new job
Count the number of conversations you have.	Use the information you gathered.	It's easier when you have already talked to the Decision Maker.	It usually happens after talking to 25 different Decision Makers.

know how long the various phases of construction usually take. This allows them to judge whether the work is moving quickly or slowly, and to make adjustments when they're needed.

Of course, it's not just in construction that measurements are important. Managers of all kinds recognize the importance of progress measurements. Some even say, "If you can't measure it, you can't manage it." That is certainly true in job search.

This last phase of the Pierson Method also includes the step of rechecking your Project Plan. You checked it before you started, but now you have more information on your personal job market. You may need to refine your plan based on the information you get from talking to friends, acquaintances, insiders, and Decision Makers.

Your final steps, of course, are interviewing, negotiating, and actually starting a new job.

Of these four steps, the most neglected is progress measurements. Many people have never used them in job search. Because they are so important to your success, I'd like to tell you a little more about them right now. And I'll tell you even more in the next chapter, "Why You Need Progress Measurements."

Progress Questions

Before you have an offer, or even an interview, how do you know if you are making progress in your search?

How much progress did you make this week?

Monitoring progress in job search is more difficult than other projects. This is partly because the search project includes some things you cannot control. It's also because measuring progress is more difficult in projects you don't do often.

Many people looking for new employment will tell you they can't measure their progress until they get an interview or a job offer. This is like a builder saying, "I can't tell you how long it will take to build your house until I finish building it." Without any progress measurements, job search is a difficult all-or-nothing game.

When you get an offer for a good job, you know you have made progress. Getting an interview for the right job in the right organization is also a clear sign of progress. But people in search usually have periods of time with no interviews—especially at the beginning.

During those dry spells, do you know if you're making progress? And if so, how much progress? If you don't know how much progress you have made, you don't know whether your plan and techniques are working.

Progress Measurements Guide the Project

**If your progress is below average,
you should change your plan and techniques.**

**If your progress is above average,
you should do more of whatever you have been doing.**

Not knowing where you stand in search (or in any project) can also be very discouraging. It's like digging a gold mine month after month by torchlight and finding nothing but rocks. You might be inches away from the richest gold strike in history. Or your tunnel might be going in the wrong direction. If you don't know which is which, you don't know whether to dig like crazy or make a U-turn. And if you don't have a clue whether you're on the right track or not, discouragement sets in.

When people in job search get discouraged, they slow down, slack off, or even quit. I've seen it again and again. All too often, someone in search is on exactly the right track and getting close to success but gives up before getting there.

Very few people know how to measure progress in job search. So far, I've rarely seen good information on how to use progress measurements in search—except at Lee Hecht Harrison, where I work. But unless you have the good luck to be laid off by a top employer, you may never get a Lee Hecht Harrison program.

CONVERSATIONS WITH 25 DECISION MAKERS

You may have figured out already what the key progress measurement is. It's conversations with the Decision Makers in the organizations on your Target List. As we discussedabove, the average person in the average search needs to talk to 25 different Decision Makers. If you have an average search and talk to two new Decision Makers every week, your search will take 12½ weeks. If you talk to about 30 friends, acquaintances, and insiders every week and ask the right questions, you will be likely to reach two Decision Makers.

When people first hear this, they sometimes think it's impossible to do all that. But it's not. At Lee Hecht Harrison, where I work now, we see up to 100,000 people a year at all salary levels and from many different backgrounds, all looking for jobs. They learn how to conduct effective searches. You can too.

That's why I've written this book for you. I've covered what you need to do and how to measure it. So stay with me. We'll get to all of it.

Because they are so useful, I've made progress measurements a central part of the Pierson Method. I'll be telling you about more of them as we go, so you can use them to see how you're doing in your search. The measurements are all simple numbers and common sense, like 25 conversations with Decision Makers. They're discussed in the next chapter, and in more detail in Chapter 11, "Keeping Score."

This chapter was an overview of the entire book. Don't worry if you don't understand all of it yet or if it doesn't make sense. I'll explain it in detail in the following chapters, and summarize it in Chapter 12.

Please read on.

ORVILLE'S JOURNAL

JESSIE REWRITES CHAPTER 2 IN FORTY-TWO WORDS

The day after I gave Jessie this chapter, she called me.

"I just read Chapter 2," she said. "This is way too hard."

"So you haven't learned all the secrets of job search success yet?" I asked. "Did you learn anything that might help?"

"Well, I learned that your daughter is good at cleaning. Can I hire her to clean my house?"

"Actually," I said, "Sarah does financial development for not-for-profits. If cleaning your house would help people understand the importance of philanthropic giving, she'd probably clean it and paint it too.

"But right now, you're unemployed. It might be better for you to get a job before you become a philanthropist. Did you learn anything else in Chapter 2?"

Jessie sighed. "You did make a good point about managing the search project. I manage my work pretty well. But I didn't even think about managing my job search.

"And now that I am thinking about it, I'm still not sure what it means. Writing lists of what I'm supposed to do every day? Keeping rejection letters in neat files? I hope not. It sounds depressing."

"It's more basic than those," I said. "It's about planning the whole job. If you were cleaning a condo, you'd make a list of the supplies and equipment you need. Decide whether it would be better to wash the walls first or the floors. And things like that."

"So in job search, that would be the Project Plan," Jessie said.

"Yes," I agreed. "It starts with deciding what kind of work you want to do, where you want to work, and what you'll say about your qualifications. Sometimes people think they should say the same things about themselves no matter what they're looking for."

"Which isn't true," said Jessie. "I always thought you've got to write your resumé for a particular kind of work. But I never thought much about what company I might like to work for. I figured it would depend on who was hiring."

"That's what a lot of people think," I said, "but it's not true. It limits your chances. It leaves too much up to the other guys, or to luck. It puts you in the position of waiting and hoping. Waiting for someone to post an opening. Waiting for them to respond to your application. And hoping they'll pick your resumé out of the pile."

"I've been doing a lot of waiting, all right," said Jessie. "Nobody answers my letters. So I wait. What else can I do?"

"Plenty," I said. "You'd get proactive. You'd take the game to them."

"Are you talking about that networking stuff that everybody talks about?" Jessie asked. "Because I think that's nuts. Going around and begging all my friends to find me a job. Finding a job is my problem, not theirs."

"I definitely don't think you should go begging. You have a lot to offer. Besides, begging for a job doesn't work," I replied. But whether you network or not isn't the point. Networking is a technique, like mopping or scrubbing. Right now, we're talking about the overall Project Plan. You can't decide what techniques to use until you've decided what game you're playing and what your game plan is. You've got to scope out the project first."

"So," Jessie said, "the key points are to know what you're looking for—both jobs and organizations—to have a proactive plan, and to measure your progress so you can tell if you're on the right track, especially if you're having a bad week?"

I smiled. "Exactly." Wow, I thought, she got it.

"Why didn't you put that in Chapter 2?" Jessie asked.

"Well," I said, "I guess you just did."

Take this one-question quiz before you start reading

Question:	**How many hours per week does an unemployed person spend on job search activities?**

❏ Over 50   ❏ 20 to 30

❏ 40 to 50   ❏ 10 to 20

❏ 30 to 40   ❏ Under 10

THE ANSWER IS ON PAGE 36.

CHAPTER THREE

Why You Need Progress Measurements

My luck has been very good for some time now, and the last time I was forced to look for a job was many years ago. I had been working for a regional career consulting firm. It was a great place to work and so successful that it grew rapidly from one office to a dozen.

But success and rapid growth can be very hard to manage. The next thing I knew, the company had very serious business problems. Nearly everyone, including me, was laid off.

You might think, "No problem, the guy's a job search expert. He found a great new job in a week." You're right about the first part. Even then I was a job search expert. At that time, I had 12 years experience in the field and had written books used by thousands of that company's clients to find new jobs. I knew exactly what I needed to do to get a new job and exactly how to do it.

I did find a great new job, but it took several months. And along the way, I had some of the same sometimes embarrassing problems that all job seekers everywhere have.

I will give myself some credit by saying that my field is a small one. Many people have never heard of career consulting companies, and that's because there aren't very many of them. To make it tougher, I had a strong preference for working at one of the largest and best.

Of course, I looked at firms of all sizes and didn't exclude any from consideration. I considered possibilities besides career consulting firms.

Nonetheless, it took longer than it needed to. One reason, I must admit, was that I didn't put in as much effort as I might have.

Did you do that quiz yet? The one on page 34? I was not in the over 50 hours a week category. Or the 40 to 50 hours a week category, or the 30 to 40, or even the 20 to 30 hour category.

The truth is that I hadn't yet thought about progress measurements at all. I was probably in the 10 to 20 hour a week category in my good weeks, and under 10 in my not-so-good weeks.

So why would a job search expert put in so little work on a job search? The best answer is that I'm human too and have the same foibles as everyone else. The amusing part is this: If job search were a simple, straightforward task, and everyone enjoyed it and was good at it, I wouldn't have a career in career consulting. This book, and the 2,500 others on the topic, wouldn't have been written.

The fact is, everyone's productivity in search tends to be low. For a host of reasons, people in search often find themselves doing less and less—and spending too much time on less productive activities. As we mentioned in the last chapter, progress measurements can help you keep your efforts at a reasonable level. You will know when you have put in a good week's work, even in those weeks when there are no results yet.

Why is productivity low? Well, as I proved when I was looking for a job, it goes beyond expertise and knowing what to do, though that is certainly important. There are a number of other factors. Let's go back to the quiz, then we'll look at what else is involved.

How Many Hours per Week Does an Unemployed Person Spend on Job Search Activities?

Correct Answer: Under 10.
Two-thirds of them spend five hours a week or less.

In a large survey, two-thirds of the unemployed people in job search reported that they spent five hours a week or less in search. Unemployed people using the Pierson Method typically put in between 25 and 35 hours per week. A few people work 40 hours a week on their job search. And some very rare individuals actually work more than 40 hours a week on search.

Of course, the most important question is how well they use their time, and I will have a great deal to say about that before you finish this book. But for the moment let's stay with the time, because five hours a week is not enough time to do much of anything.

Those same people who work only five hours a week on job search normally put in 40 (or 50 or 60) hours a week at their regular jobs. Spending only five hours a week in job search is a huge drop in productivity. It's pretty close to going on vacation. But if you're unemployed, finding a new job is very important, and you have nothing else to do. So let's ask the obvious question: Why do unemployed people spend so little time on job search?

Low Productivity in Search
Why do unemployed people spend so little time on something so important?

Over the years, whenever I've dug into the reasons why unemployed people don't work very hard in job search, I always get the same list of reasons. The truth is that there are numerous barriers to productivity in search. Some particularly affect the unemployed. Some affect everyone.

It is important for you to be aware of these so you can set up a plan to keep your productivity high in spite of the barriers. In my experience, the single most important reason that people take too long to find a new job is that they get discouraged and slacken their efforts. Or just plain give up.

Beyond slowing down or stopping, people often just don't know what works in a job search and what does not. What you do with your search time is also important, since some techniques work much better than others. But the first thing is to consistently put time and effort into your search, even when you are not getting immediate results. And even if you feel discouraged.

Let's look at five of the most common reasons why people put in less time and effort than they should. Several of these barriers slowed me down the last time I was looking. If you're a normal human being, chances are that some—or all—of them will affect you too. But they don't have to stop you. Take a look at the list below.

The Five Biggest Barriers to Productivity in Job Search
(These are why you need progress measurements.)

1. The rejection syndrome
2. Emotional stress
3. Working solo
4. Lowered self-esteem and confidence
5. No plan or the wrong plan

---

1. THE REJECTION SYNDROME

Everyone knows that job search involves rejection. Not just once or twice, but again and again. Employers tell you that you're the wrong person. That they're not taking applications. That you're underqualified, overqualified, undereducated, too inexperienced, or too late.

In fact, the entire search is nothing but rejection. After all, the first time a Decision Maker offers you a great job instead of rejecting you, your search is over. So the entire search is rejection after rejection, until finally one organization does not reject you.

When normal people are rejected again and again, they get discouraged, then depressed. People who feel depressed, discouraged, or "down" don't do very much. In the extreme case (which needs medical treatment), depressed people do not even get out of bed in the morning.

When someone doesn't work on their search, things get even worse, and even more depressing. Which leads to even less work. Unless the person is able to break out of this cycle, the search flounders—or just plain stops. This is the rejection syndrome.

But It's Not All Bad; Here's How to Turn It Around

One career author once turned the idea of rejection around in a very useful way. He said that when you are in search, you should take a sheet of graph paper and put an X in one of the little squares every time you are rejected. Your job is to fill the sheet with Xs. Before you fill the sheet, you will have a new job.

This is actually a crude progress measurement. Your job in job search is to go out every day and get rejected. Once you get enough rejections out of the way, you will find that one really good acceptance. Then the search is over.

If you knew how many Xs you needed to chalk up, the search would be easier to deal with, wouldn't it? Then, at least, you'd know where the end was, and even if it was a long way off, you'd know that you were getting closer.

Of course, no one can tell you exactly how many it will take. But the Pierson Method shows that the average person in search is "rejected"— or at least not hired—by 24 Decision Makers before being hired by number 25. Your number could be higher. Or lower. But 25 is the average. More on that in Chapter 11. For now, let's look at the other four reasons why productivity in search is low.

2. EMOTIONAL STRESS

Emotional reactions in job search often go beyond depression to frustration, anger, anxiety, and many others. With people who are unemployed and under financial pressure, the reasons for this stress are obvious. If it started with being caught in a downsizing, that can add another level of emotional reaction.

People who are currently employed can also have emotional stress. Often they're looking for a new job because of problems in their current work situation. This can cause a high stress level and many of the same emotions. They also have to worry about whether the boss will find out that they're looking. And how to find time to conduct a search.

Whether you're employed or unemployed, negative emotions can interfere with getting the search project done. They can also produce negative communications that can damage your search. Speaking negatively of one's current or last employer is a common example of this problem—and a good way *not* to get hired.

3. WORKING SOLO

Job search is a much more individual and entrepreneurial activity than working in a regular job. There are no organizational resources to support you. You're on your own, with no boss, coworkers, or subordinates to assist you in figuring it out, getting it organized, and getting it done. It's just you.

Most jobs structure your time with regular work hours, deadlines, and the like. In job search you have to manage your own time—and figure out the best ways to use it. Time management can be an even bigger problem for employed people, because they have to balance the demands of job search with work and other demands.

The Job Search Work Teams in the Special Section of this book can help break through this barrier. You can work with a team, rather than go it alone, to get your search done faster. In fact, the team approach helps with all five barriers.

If you don't have a team and don't want to create one, talking to someone informally about your search will also help. This will work best if your partner has also read this book so they understand job search.

4. LOWERED SELF-ESTEEM AND CONFIDENCE

Feelings caused by job loss or rejection in search can make it difficult to hang on to your self-confidence. This is particularly true of unemployed people who identified with their former title or role. Which is most of us. You may feel: "I was a vice president, and now I'm a nobody." Or, "I was a breadwinner, and now I'm a drain on the family finances." Employed people may suffer lower self-esteem and self-confidence because of an unpleasant work situation.

Low self-esteem and confidence make for poor interviewing. And make it harder to keep the search going and get an interview in the first place. After all, a search is about telling people how good you are, which is hard to do if your confidence is down.

5. NO PLAN OR THE WRONG PLAN

As we saw in the last chapter, both the employed and unemployed often approach search with a weak plan or none at all. While "winging it" sometimes works, it is not the best way to get good results in job search, or anything else.

Overcoming the Barriers

Be aware of them.

Create a Project Plan, check it and use it.

Track your progress with numerical measures.

Try a Job Search Work Team.

You may have noticed that these barriers are mostly psychological, internal barriers rather than barriers in the external world. But they are real. These psychological factors often affect productivity and can result in people investing too little time in search—and investing it in the wrong places.

Being aware of these barriers—of the things that can work against you—and finding ways to deal with them is essential. This is why I put them near the beginning of the book.

Obviously there are ways of addressing some of these barriers individually. Taking care of yourself, practicing good health habits, establishing a routine, talking to supportive people, seeking out counseling for more severe stress—the list goes on and on. You should do those things when they are needed.

But the truth is that some barriers cannot be eliminated. Rejection, for example, is part of the game. While you do not necessarily have to feel rejected every time you get a turndown, turndowns won't go away until you land a new job.

The real challenge is to keep on track despite the barriers. Unemployed people need to treat job search as a job and make a systematic effort every week until they succeed. Employed people looking for new employment elsewhere often have difficulty finding the time to conduct a search. This makes it even more important that they use what time they do have in the most productive ways possible.

According to the Pierson Method, the best way is to create a Project Plan and prepare effectively. Then follow your plan and measure your progress toward a new job. Since you might have some weeks when you feel discouraged, your measurements need to be objective— numbers, in other words—not just vague ideas about whether you did well or not so well.

MEASURE YOUR PROGRESS

Progress measurements are very useful in overcoming all of the barriers to productivity in search. If week after week you have no way of knowing if you're moving closer to your goal, your morale and your productivity go down. With a system for tracking progress, you can have a sense of accomplishment every day. Instead of focusing on rejections, you can look at the progress you've made. At the end of each week, you know you have done a good job in search, even if you've had no offers yet.

If you're unemployed, you may even get a week's worth of job search done in four days. If so, I suggest that you take a three-day weekend. You earned it. You know you deserve it because of your progress measurements. It can help reduce the stress and get you ready for another week in search.

Teaming up with one or more other people while you are in search can also be very useful. They'll help keep you objective and on the straight and narrow path toward a new job. And it surely doesn't hurt to have a friend or two working with you—or at least standing beside you—while you work on this tough job.

The Special Section on Job Search Work Teams at the end of this book shows you several different ways to team up with others in search—formally with a team or informally with a friend. Whether you work with a team or not, you need to understand just how the hiring game is played. That's the topic of the next chapter.

ORVILLE'S JOURNAL

JESSIE, BEN, AND I DISCUSS PROGRESS MEASUREMENTS, THE MAGNET MAN, AND THE MOVERS

I was weeding the garden a few days after we'd discussed Chapter 2, when Jessie came walking up to the fence.

"Orville," she offered, "you sure said a mouthful about the barriers to productivity in job search."

"Was that helpful?" I asked.

"I don't know about helpful," she said, "but it was true. Your book says people in job search are depressed. Then you make us more depressed. But you're right, I'm not doing much in my search these days. And you missed a few reasons why people slack off in search."

"Really?" I had put only a few reasons in the book, since most people don't want to talk about them. But Jessie did want to talk, so I figured I'd listen. "What did I miss?"

"People just plain don't know how to do a job search. There's a million books out there and they all say something different," she replied. "The resumé is the key. Don't use a resumé. You've got to network. The Internet is the way. It just goes on and on.

"And the more discouraging it gets, the more I have other things to do," she continued. "Sometimes it's just real important to sweep the walk, clean the kitchen, do anything except that lousy job search."

"I'd call that avoidance," Ben said. He had walked up behind her and was now leaning on the fence next to Jessie.

"It's very common," I said, "especially for people who got laid off. The workplace has been nuts. They need a rest. And now they're supposed to go out and get rejected in a job search? You can't blame them for avoiding it sometimes."

"And then," said Ben, "there's the skill problem. You're supposed to be a resumé writer. A great interviewer. An Internet genius."

"This whole thing is just getting more and more depressing," Jessie said. "What's the solution, Orville?"

"He already told you, Jessica," snapped Ben. "Progress measurements and planning. You have to plan it. Nobody plans a job search. Nobody has progress measurements. I think he's right."

"And I think you should stay out of it, Ben," shot Jessie. "You haven't looked for a job for years. What do you know about it?"

"Jessie," I said, "let me say something else about the rejection part, where the discouragement sets in." It looked like they were heading for another argument, so I thought I'd try changing the subject.

"In job search," I continued, "people often feel rejected. And, of course, sometimes they are rejected. But other times they do the rejecting. Have you rejected any employers?"

"No," she said.

"Yes, you have," Ben interjected. "What about the Ajax Group? You wouldn't even talk to them. And what about Magnet Man?"

"The Ajax job was half my last salary. And Magnet Man? You've got to be kidding! That was multilevel marketing!"

"They were lousy jobs. Definitely not for you. But Orville is right. They didn't reject you. You rejected both of them."

Jessie didn't look very happy about being told again how right Orville was. So I jumped in again. "Can I tell you a story?" I asked. I really wanted to help her get over being so discouraged.

"Okay," said Jessie, a little doubtful.

"Suppose that you and Ben were moving. So the movers come. The two of you go out for the day. While you're gone the movers pack things up. When you and Ben return, the furniture is on the truck and the other stuff is packed in 25 boxes, all lined up on the front lawn. The boxes are unlabeled but each one has a number on it—one to 25."

"Unlabeled?" said Jessie. "Boy, is that a lousy moving company."

"It's a story," Ben said.

"But Jessie," I continued, "you realize that your walking shoes have been packed and you want to wear them. So you start looking for them. You look in the first box. Not there. The second box. Not there. The third, the fourth, the fifth. Not there.

"Finally, you find them in box number 11. Did the first 10 boxes reject you?"

Jessie actually smiled a little. "Okay," she said, "I get it."

"Why didn't she talk to the packers?" Ben asked. "They know where the shoes are. Or at least they can eliminate some boxes."

"Ben," Jessie said, "sometimes you're a real piece of work."

"He's on the right track," I said, "and so are you, Jessie."

"Okay," said Jessie, "on to Chapter 4."

FACT:	**People who hire people (Decision Makers) always use one of these three hiring scenarios:**

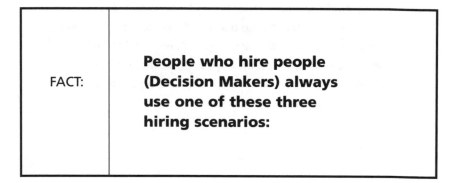

1 The Applicant Pool

2 The Created Position

3 The Known Candidate

CHAPTER FOUR

How Hiring Really Happens

My brother-in-law was born in Togo. I must admit that before my sister Ruth married him, I didn't know where Togo was. I knew it was in Africa, but they didn't teach much about Africa when I was in school.

Anyway, when Ruth told us she was marrying a man from Togo, I found a map and checked it out. In case you don't already know, Togo is one of the Rhode Islands of Africa—a very small country in that huge continent. It's on Africa's western coast, in that big notch on the coastline, so if you sat on the beach in Togo, you'd be looking south at the Atlantic Ocean.

I've never been to Togo, but I understand that they speak a number of languages, in addition to the official language, French. If I were going to go there, I'd have a lot to learn, in addition to French. And if I wanted to live there and earn a living, I'd need to learn even more. The same may be true of you.

Suppose, for example, that you were moving there and wanted to start a business—a nice little café offering sandwiches and coffee. Let's assume that you speak French, but, like me, you have never been to Togo, or even to Africa. Before you made the move and started the business, it would be smart to find out how the Togolese people do things—especially what they eat and what they're willing to pay for it. Do they go to restaurants at all? Do they like sandwiches and coffee?

In the same way, before you start your job search, you should consider the world of Decision Makers, the people who manage organizations (or departments) and hire people. If you have been a Decision Maker yourself, thinking about how you hired people is a great start. If you've been trained in interviewing and selection, you probably do it better than the average Decision Maker, who was never taught anything about hiring. If you're one of the thousands of Decision Makers out there who were never trained in how to do hiring, you might ask whether others do it the same way you do.

If you've never hired people, then it's like moving to Togo—you're operating in a foreign country. You need to understand how Decision Makers think and act. You need to know what pressures push them to do things in certain ways. Most of all, you need to know how they handle the job of hiring a new employee. Once you understand how they play the game, you can adjust your game plan accordingly.

That's what we are going to do in this chapter: understand the hiring game, and how it's really played. Let's start with who does what.

Human Resources and the Decision Maker
**The decision to hire you will be made
by your next boss (the Decision Maker) —
not the Human Resources department.**

When you are looking for a new job, the Decision Maker is the person who will be your next boss. Other members of the department or team may also be involved in the hiring process. But the Decision Makers have the final say on who their employees are. In larger organizations, Human Resources (HR) professionals may assist the Decision Maker. But in the end, it is the Decision Maker, your next boss, who will make the decision to hire you.

In some organizations, the HR department is a trusted partner of the Decision Maker in the hiring process. They assist the manager by locating candidates, interviewing and screening them, and recommending a few. Then the Decision Maker does the final interviews and makes a decision. When hiring is done this way, Decision Makers may still add their own candidates at any stage in the process.

In other organizations, the Decision Maker may not believe that HR understands their work well enough to assist in hiring. Or HR simply may not be set up to help Decision Makers fill all openings at all levels. There are many organizations where the HR department doesn't even know that hiring is happening until the Decision Maker tells them it's done—and asks them to do the paperwork on a new employee.

However it happens, the key person in the hiring process is always the Decision Maker, your next boss.

Sometimes people in search assume that the HR department has all the power in hiring everyone. This is just plain wrong. Unless you want a job in the Human Resources department, HR is not your best starting point. Smaller organizations may not even have an HR department—but they might have some very good jobs.

You should plan your search project based on how you believe Decision Makers do things, just as you would plan your Togolese business based on how the Togolese people do things. If you understand how hiring *really* happens, you will be way ahead of the game. If not, your search may not work well. Which is why I want to talk to you about it before going into detail on the Project Plan.

THE THREE WAYS THAT HIRING HAPPENS

There are only three different ways Decision Makers hire new people. Over the years, I have talked to many career counselors and job search consultants and hundreds—possibly thousands—of people in job search about how hiring happens. Many of those people were themselves Decision Makers with a lot of hiring experience. So far, no one has come up with a description of how hiring happens that does not fit into one of these three scenarios:

1. The Applicant Pool
2. The Created Position
3. Tapping a Known Candidate

People always recognize the three, especially Scenario #3, Tapping a Known Candidate. They have been hired that way, hired people that way, or seen people hired that way. For most of us, Scenario #3 is the best and easiest way to go.

While there are many variations of each scenario, all hiring happens in one of these three ways. They are all commonsense ways of doing the job of hiring. They work well for the Decision Makers using them. Candidates who understand them find better jobs faster. In the rest of this chapter, we will take a look at each of the three, starting with the Applicant Pool approach.

How Hiring Happens, Scenario #1
THE APPLICANT POOL

1. There is an open position.
2. A pool of candidates is collected and screened.
3. The Decision Maker interviews the top candidates.
4. The Decision Maker selects one of the candidates.

About one-quarter of all hiring happens this way.

Scenario #1: The Applicant Pool

To understand this scenario, picture an organization—let's call it Central Dynamics, Inc.—that has divided the work into 100 jobs and has an employee in each of those 100. You can see this as an organization chart. There is one box on top of the chart, the president. We'll call her Gail. Below that are three boxes, the department managers, Frank, Manuel, and Susan. Frank has 16 people in his department, Manuel has 40, and Susan has 40—each with job titles and their own box on the chart.

Central Dynamics is not downsizing—it needs all 100 people to get the work done. If the head count gets down to 99, several people are carrying an extra load. If it got down to 95 employees, it would be in danger of failing to meet its contractual obligations. So keeping all 100 jobs filled with the right people is very important.

Each of the 100 boxes represents an essential piece of work and each box has a name in it—the person who has that job now. The hiring scenario begins when one day a name disappears from a box. Someone retires, quits, or moves on. Now there is an empty box on the organizational chart—a job opening.

As usual, Central Dynamics starts by filling the opening with an internal person. But doing that just creates another empty box somewhere else on the chart. When the game of musical chairs ends, there are still 99 people and one job opening. As it happens, the opening is in Susan's department this time.

To fill that opening, Susan, who is the Decision Maker in this case, has to look outside. Wanting a lot of choices, she collects a large applicant pool. This can be done in a number of different ways. Maybe she uses the Internet or newspaper ads or a staffing firm. If Central Dynamics was a larger organization, Susan might get help from the Human Resources department in finding and screening candidates— but Susan would still be the Decision Maker.

Next, this large applicant pool has to be screened. There are 952 resumés. Susan is extra busy right now because she's missing a person, and the president just gave her a special project. She doesn't have HR help, so she asks her administrative assistant to narrow the 952 down to six. The next day there are six resumés on Susan's desk.

Were these six the best in the stack? Maybe. If the assistant knew the job to be filled very well and reviewed all 952 resumés carefully, then yes, Susan got the best. But suppose the assistant didn't know the job well, had to help Susan with the special project, do her ordinary work, and also screen 952 resumés in 24 hours. Then what?

Anyway, however the screening happened, Susan, the Decision Maker, invites those six finalists to come in for an interview. She does the interviewing herself and makes the final selection—maybe involving other people in the department, or maybe not. That candidate is hired and their name entered into the empty box on the organization chart. The opening is filled. Central Dynamics, Inc. is back to 100 employees. Susan breathes a sigh of relief.

This is the Applicant Pool scenario of how hiring happens. Let's look at why Decision Makers use it and what it means for you.

Decision Makers Use the Applicant Pool Scenario Because:

They have to.

It gives them a wider range of choices.

The other two scenarios didn't work.

It's the only way they know.

One reason Decision Makers use this approach is very simple: Some organizations have a policy requiring it. Sometimes there are government regulations requiring it. Of course, some managers are famous for circumventing policies they don't like. But some do follow the policy, using the Applicant Pool method even though they would rather not.

Another reason Decision Makers go this way is that they want to have a wide range of candidates to choose from. They may want to foster diversity in the workplace to get the work done better. Or they may just believe that having a lot of choices ensures getting a better employee. Managerial and executive jobs may be filled this way, using recruiters to assist.

A third reason—possibly the most common one—is that the Decision Maker already tried one of the other two scenarios and it didn't work. Or didn't work well enough.

Decision makers often start with Scenario #3, Tapping a Known Candidate. But if they don't know of a good candidate and can't find one by asking around, they'll probably move to the Applicant Pool scenario. When the Applicant Pool scenario of hiring is the Decision Maker's last choice, jobs found this way may be the "leftovers," the less desirable jobs.

However, the Applicant Pool scenario is a traditional way of doing hiring. Organizations can and do find good new employees this way. Some Decision Makers use it simply because they believe it is the right way—or because it's the only way they know.

What the Applicant Pool Scenario Means for the Candidate

Competition.
A formal process.
The resumé is king.

The one thing that is most certain for you is that there is a lot of competition for Applicant Pool jobs. The larger the applicant pool, the more competition there is. Internet postings or ads in the paper draw a lot of people, especially if the job or organization is a good one. In weak job markets, ads and postings draw even larger numbers. So if the Decision Maker is using this method, watch out. You may be one of hundreds of candidates.

In collecting and screening large numbers of people in applicant pools, employers rely heavily on resumés. To get into the game, you need to have a resumé including whatever key words they are searching for. If your resumé has the right key words and qualifications, it gets pulled out of their resumé database or pile of paper resumés. If your resumé contains one line that someone finds worrisome, you will probably be screened out.

In this scenario, your resumé is king. If you have just the right background and it's described well in the resumé, you've got a pretty good chance of getting a call for an interview. If your background and resumé are not in the top 10 percent, your odds drop. After all, they will only interview the few who look best on paper.

IT'S ABOUT RESUMÉS, NOT PEOPLE

The Applicant Pool scenario is a formal one, based initially on resumés alone. Only if your resumé survives the screening do you get a chance to talk to someone. You may be a better *person* for the job than the owner of the best resumé, but the screening process doesn't consider people—it's all about words on paper. Only at the end do people talk to people. And then, it's a formal interview—not a casual, friendly conversation.

The Applicant Pool scenario works best for candidates looking for the same kind of work they are currently doing or did in their last job. It works best for those candidates who also have strong credentials that can easily be displayed on paper, and for those who are good at resumé writing and formal interviewing. For others, Scenario #3, Tapping a Known Candidate, is usually the way to go.

All of this adds up to the fact that the Applicant Pool approach is difficult for most of us. Luckily, it accounts for only about a quarter of the hiring. The next one, the Created Position, also asks a lot of the candidate—but the competition is low to nonexistent. It accounts for only a small percentage of hiring, but it could be the route to your ideal job.

How Hiring Happens, Scenario #2
THE CREATED POSITION

1. You identify organizational needs.
2. You discuss those needs with the Decision Maker.
3. You suggest meeting the needs by creating a new job.
4. The Decision Maker creates a new job and gives it to you.

Less than 5 percent of hiring happens this way.
But this could be the way you get your ideal job.

Scenario #2: The Created Position

In Scenario #2 you approach a Decision Maker and convince them that hiring you will produce enough additional profit or cost saving to justify your salary. If the Decision Maker is convinced that the benefit exceeds the cost—and can afford to pay your salary—you're hired.

In this scenario, there doesn't need to be a job opening for hiring to occur, because a new one is added. Central Dynamics goes from 100 to 101 employees. You are hired when there is no opening.

Here's how this scenario works: You identify what the organization needs, usually by talking to people below the Decision Maker's level. You then meet with the Decision Maker to discuss these needs and how you can help. You suggest to the Decision Maker that hiring the right person is a good way to meet some important needs. You show them how you are the right person. Finally, assuming that the arguments are strong and necessary approvals gained, a position is created—just for you.

Suppose, for example, that our friends at Central Dynamics have had more and more computer problems as their computer systems expanded. They have used some very expensive computer consultants, but the problems are getting more expensive—and not going away. You are a strong computer person. You hear about the problems from some Central Dynamics employees. One of them, Charlie, works in Frank's department, the financial and data processing department.

Charlie explains the whole situation to you and introduces you to Frank. You convince Frank that you could solve the problems if you worked there. You and Frank write up a job description. Frank takes it to the president, Gail, who approves it and congratulates Frank on solving the problem and saving money. You get hired into a job that was literally made for you.

Easy to do? No. A common way of finding a new job? No. Only a small percentage of hiring happens in this way, probably less than 5 percent. So why am I taking the time to cover it? For two reasons:

First, because it's like hitting the job jackpot. It's harder to do, but if you do it, it can be a great career move, because the job is built around your skills and interests. I don't expect you to find an opportunity for a created job very often. But if one comes up, I don't want you to miss it. Watch for this possibility in smaller and growing organizations, in higher level positions, or if you have unique skills.

Second, because I want you to know all three hiring scenarios. Even though fewer people find jobs this way, it *does* happen. It's one of the three, and it's distinctly different from the other two.

Notice that the Created Position scenario is completely different from the Applicant Pool. In that scenario, an opening exists and candidates are recruited to fill it. In the Created Position scenario, the job seeker pursues organizations that *have no current openings*. You arrive first and the opening is created later, tailored to the skills and interests of the only candidate—you.

So please keep your eyes open. You might see an opportunity for a Created Position as you conduct a search for jobs being filled using the other two scenarios. Here is what it does for Decision Makers, and for you.

Why Decision Makers Use the Created Position

It solves a problem.
It can make their job easier.

Decision Makers use it because it solves problems for them. The problems may include costs that are too high, revenue or profits that are too low, or anything else.

Suppose, for example, that a Decision Maker who manages a large sales force has spent a great deal of money on outside sales trainers. The training is effective and necessary, but the training company is constantly changing trainers, so the trainers leave just when they are getting acquainted with the sales force and the products. And the cost is very high.

Now suppose that you're a sales trainer who can do that training as an employee for less than half the cost of the outside training firm. If you and the manager like each other, you have a good chance of having a position created for you.

Creating the new position makes the manager's job easier, since sales training is no longer a worry. With sales training working well, sales go up. Because your salary is lower than the outside company, costs go down. And you may pick up one or two of the sales manager's other duties as well. So the Decision Maker is happy with the arrangement.

At a higher level, new management jobs may be created in expanding organizations. On the other hand, if you are just out of college, you are less likely to have a position created for you. But you never know.

What the Created Position Scenario Means for You

A really great job, tailor-made for you.
You must take the initiative.

Because you negotiate the content of the job, including the "one or two other duties" the Decision Maker wants you to do, the job is built around your strengths and interests, like tailor-made clothes. On the other hand, you must take a great deal of initiative, especially in locating the organization with needs you can fill. Scenario #3, Tapping a Known Candidate, is easier for you and for the Decision Maker—which is why it is so popular, accounting for most hiring.

How Hiring Happens, Scenario #3
TAPPING A KNOWN CANDIDATE

1. The Decision Maker knows of some qualified people.
2. A position opens up.
3. The Decision Maker hires one of the known candidates.

Sometimes the Decision Maker goes through the motions of collecting and screening a candidate pool, then hires a preselected, known candidate.

About three quarters of all hiring happens like this.

Scenario #3: Tapping a Known Candidate

Decision Makers often put other things before skills and experience. If you were the Decision Maker, would you prefer average skills in a person you liked or outstanding skills in a person you couldn't stand having near you? Would you rather hire a highly skilled person who shows no interest in the job or a less skilled person who is enthusiastic? Someone less skilled that you were sure you could trust, or someone more skilled that you weren't sure about?

While skills are important, they are often not the first consideration. Real Decision Makers are also real people. Like the rest of us, they usually prefer interested, enthusiastic people that they have some reason to like and trust. And they are often willing to accept a lower skill level to get someone like that. After all, people who aren't interested may not come to work at all, especially on Fridays and Mondays. And people who are very interested develop skills quickly.

In the Tapping a Known Candidate scenario, the Decision Maker knows a candidate before there is an opening. There is no need to announce the position or collect a large pool of applicants. Instead, the Decision Maker simply fills the job with a person that they met before the opening happened—someone they had in mind all along.

Remember Susan, the Decision Maker at Central Dynamics? As an experienced department head with 40 employees, she knows that she has employee turnover. In fact, she knows that her turnover rate will require her to hire about four employees a year, one every 90 days. And she knows that being shorthanded causes problems. So will she wait until someone leaves to look for candidates? No way. She's smart. She is quietly on the lookout for candidates all the time.

As an example of how this scenario works, suppose that Susan has a cousin named Fred. She likes him and knows that he can do the job. Susan asks Fred if he's interested in working for her. Fred says yes. The next time an opening occurs, there is no applicant pool—Fred gets the job.

When an opening comes up, she may tell Fred he has to wait a few weeks while she posts it. Then she posts it internally, collects an external applicant pool, and screens and interviews people. She keeps records of all of this. But she is not serious about those candidates. She's doing it because there's a policy that says she is supposed to. In the end she hires Fred, as she had planned to do all along. In this case, what looked like an Applicant Pool scenario really was not. It was a known candidate, Fred.

In another version of the Known Candidate scenario, Fred is not a cousin, but a trusted friend of Susan's. He is not interested in working for her. Susan knows she may have an opening coming up, so she asks Fred if he knows anyone. Fred suggests an acquaintance, José. Susan and José meet. She likes him, and when the next job comes open, she immediately hires José. This can happen even when Fred does not know José well.

Another way Susan might find candidates is to ask her employees. They know what it takes to succeed in the job. They understand the organization and know what kind of boss Susan is. As current employees of Susan's, they have an interest in finding someone who will work out.

Susan favors candidates proposed by a current employee, especially an employee she likes. Employees may propose candidates before the opening is announced or even before it exists. These known candidates can step into the job as soon as it comes open.

Why Decision Makers Prefer Tapping a Known Candidate

It's fast, easy, and inexpensive.
They feel safer and more comfortable.
It just seems to happen by itself.

Most Decision Makers behave like Susan. If they happen to meet someone who might be a good candidate, they will certainly make note of it. When they later have an opening, why not call that person and ask them in for an interview? If the person qualifies, they don't need to look further. It's taken care of. Tapping a Known Candidate can be very quick and easy for the Decision Maker.

Any Decision Maker who wants to collect an applicant pool needs to pay for an ad or an Internet listing, wait for the responses to come in, screen hundreds of resumés, then conduct telephone screening interviews and final in-person interviews. This is a lot of extra work.

Or the Decision Maker could have a staffing firm do all this work—for a fee of 15 to 33 percent of the annual salary of the position to be filled. This could amount to $6,000 for a $40,000 job, or $50,000 for a $150,000 management position.

All of the Applicant Pool hiring methods take time, energy, and money. Decision Makers like Susan don't have the time or energy, especially when they're shorthanded. Susan and her boss both like it when she saves money. It's easy to see why she might prefer to hire her cousin Fred, Fred's acquaintance, José, someone recommended by a current employee, or someone she happened to meet last week at a social event. Any of these would be a great deal faster and less expensive than Applicant Pool approaches.

In fact, the idea of hiring acquaintances of current employees works so well that some organizations offer $500, $1,000, or more to employees who bring in a candidate who is successfully hired. Compared to that agency fee of $6,000, a thousand bucks is a bargain.

Decision Makers are also more comfortable with Tapping a Known Candidate. This comfort can be even more important than cost and time. Imagine yourself as the Decision Maker. Your hiring decisions, right or wrong, are noticed by everyone, including your boss. Your success depends on having the people you hire succeed.

If you hire a candidate you found on the Internet, you can check their references and experience, but how do you know that they're not usually in a bad mood? Or that they're people who cannot get along with their boss? Or even that they might be cocaine users? They could look very good at a one-hour interview and very bad later.

On the other hand, most people would feel comfortable that a friend of a friend would be a good employee. You trust Fred, and Fred tells you that José is okay. It's simple: José is worth hiring. It's a good bet because you trust Fred. But if this same José showed up as a candidate through the Internet, well, that's got the same risks as Internet dating, doesn't it?

And the same is true of someone referred by a current employee. Most Decision Makers are more comfortable with a friend of a friend than with a "stranger" who responded to an ad or Internet posting.

For many Decision Makers, enough candidates seem to "show up" through these informal means that they never have to pay money or spend much time looking. It just seems to happen by itself.

All in all, Known Candidates are a very good deal for Decision Makers. Being one is very good for you—and not difficult, as you will soon see.

What Being a Known Candidate Means for You

Limited competition, maybe none.
It's not difficult.
Informal discussions can replace formal interviews.
You talk to Decision Makers *before* they have openings.

If you are a Known Candidate, you have much less competition than you would in the Applicant Pool scenario. If you meet the right Decision Maker today and they have an opening in the next week or two, you might be the only candidate. There is no large applicant pool—it includes only the few people smart enough to find a way to meet the Decision Maker.

There are numerous ways you can become a Known Candidate. People often do it by accident. They happen to meet someone who happens to know someone else who knows the Decision Maker. If you have found jobs more than a couple of times in your life, maybe it has already happened to you. It doesn't have to be an accident. You can do it on purpose, which is actually part of the Pierson Method.

If you meet the Decision Maker on an informal basis, when there is no job opening, there's little pressure. The two of you can have a casual conversation and get acquainted. If there is later a formal interview with the same Decision Maker, it feels different because you have already met. And the Decision Maker treats you differently if you are "a friend of Fred's."

There is good evidence that these informal means of hiring Known Candidates is how about 75 percent of hiring happens. This is very significant since many people think the main thing in a job search is finding openings or finding out "who is hiring." In fact, talking to people who are NOT hiring right now is usually the best way to look for a new job.

THE CANDIDATE COMES FIRST, THE JOB OPENING IS LATER

Scenario #1, the Applicant Pool, is very different from Scenarios #2 and #3. In Scenario #1, the job opening comes first, then candidates are located. In Scenarios #2 and #3, the candidate is on the scene first and the opening happens later. The candidate gets acquainted with the right Decision Makers—or at least is known to them—prior to the opening.

Most people looking for jobs put all of their time into looking for job openings. They search for openings on the Internet and in the help wanted ads. They ask around about which organizations have openings. In doing this, they limit themselves to Scenario #1, the Applicant Pool—or about 25 percent of the job market.

I am going to say this again, because it is one of the most important things I say in this book. Most people set up a job search to look for job openings. As we saw in Scenarios #2 and #3, most hiring decisions happen *before* there is an opening. You need to talk to people who are NOT hiring right now.

How Hiring Happens:
COMPARING THE THREE SCENARIOS

In Scenario # 1, the Applicant Pool, the job opening comes first, then candidates are located.

In Scenarios # 2 and 3, the Created Position and the Known Candidate, the candidate is on the scene before the opening occurs.

In job search, most people concentrate on locating openings, rather than working upstream of the opening. This limits them to Scenario 1, and they miss out on the majority of the opportunities.

Talking to Decision Makers before they have an opening is the best way to cover all three hiring scenarios.

Pursue the Decision Maker, before There Is a Job Opening

If you want to be really effective, you should target specific organizations, whether they have openings right now or not. Sooner or later everyone has an opening. You want the right job, not simply the first one that comes up. If you are effective at getting your message across to the right Decision Makers *before* they have an opening, your competition is lower and your odds of more quickly finding a really good job go up. You are using Scenarios #2 and #3, the Created Position and the Known Candidate.

Finding new employment is not just about pursuing job openings. It is about pursuing the right Decision Makers at the right organizations. This is actually more efficient. It also increases your chances of getting a job you truly like because you are focused on organizations you like, not just on the ones that have openings right now.

THE PIERSON METHOD COVERS ALL THREE
HIRING SCENARIOS

An effective job search takes all three scenarios into account. The key in all three is talking to Decision Makers. In the Applicant Pool, you get to talk to the Decision Maker only if you get through the application and screening process. In the other two, you get in touch with Decision Makers before they have openings.

In fact, the best time to talk to a Decision Maker is *just before* the opening occurs. That way the Decision Maker will remember you when the opening happens. Assuming that you are qualified, you will be the easy and convenient hiring choice. If you are introduced by someone who knows the Decision Maker in any way, your odds go up even more.

After an opening is announced, you should certainly talk to the Decision Maker if you can. But the increased competition makes everything more difficult. Now everyone wants to talk to that Decision Maker.

The catch, of course, is that you don't know when the opening will happen. It could be tomorrow. It could be several months from now. Even the Decision Maker may not know. So what you need to do is systematically contact Decision Makers. The more of them you get in touch with, the more likely that one of them will have an opening soon. When one does, your odds are good because you are a part of a small group of candidates. With luck, you're the only candidate.

When talking about finding new work, nearly everyone quickly moves to a discussion of who is hiring, where the openings are, or how good (or bad) the job market is.

SOONER OR LATER, EVERY DECISION MAKER
HAS AN OPENING

In my opinion, who has the openings is an irrelevant question. Or worse, it is a problem, since asking it misleads people. Sooner or later every Decision Maker will have an opening. When that moment comes, those who have already met that Decision Maker (or at least gotten their message to him or her) will have an advantage. Possibly an insurmountable advantage.

So the core of the search project is getting your message to the right Decision Makers, preferably *before* they have an opening.

How Hiring Usually Happens

The average job search includes conversations with 25 Decision Makers.

They have no opening when you first talk to them.

Later, one of them has an opening and hires you.

How many Decision Makers will you need to contact? According to research done by Lee Hecht Harrison, the global career services firm I work for, the average number is 25. Naturally, some lucky people get hired by the first Decision Maker they talk to. Some others may need to talk to 30 or 40. But the average is around 25. We'll look at this more in Chapter 9, "How Many Fish Are in That Pond?" and Chapter 11, "Keeping Score."

This might seem a daunting task, but it's not really complicated. You need a good solid Project Plan to be sure that you are contacting the right Decision Makers in the right way with the right message. It's not about sending them resumés. It's not about filing applications. It's about informal contact.

The key to effective search is a Project Plan. I have come to believe that a Project Plan—and especially the Target List it includes—is as important as a resumé. Which is why we'll get started working on it in the next chapter.

ORVILLE'S JOURNAL

WE HAVE A HEATED DISCUSSION ABOUT HOW HIRING HAPPENS

I was sitting in my living room, writing on my laptop, when there was excited knocking on the door. Before I could get to the door, Ben rushed in, waving the draft of my job hunting book. This book. Jessie was behind him, but not moving as fast.

"Orville, this chapter is great. Really great. It's got to be the best chapter, except maybe for Chapter 12." Ben was usually a quiet, thoughtful person, but today he was on a roll.

"Going after Decision Makers—going after targeted organizations, not just openings, that's exactly right! The three scenarios are great! Right on the money! The bit about 25 Decision Makers is really—..."

Jessie had heard enough. "Oh, shut up, Ben," she snapped. "Whose job search is this? Last time I checked, you still had a job. You haven't been unemployed since 1998. And while we're at it, why are you reading my whole dang book? We're supposed to be talking about Chapter 4, but you're talking about Chapter 12. What are you going to do, find another job? You already have one."

Ben looked suddenly deflated. "Well, if I had this book in '98, I would have found a job faster," he said quietly.

I figured it was time for me to say something. There's a heated job hunting discussion going on in my living room, and I am, after all, a job hunting expert. "What did you think of Chapter Four, Jessie?" I asked.

"Actually," she replied, "I thought it was pretty good, too. Only I'm still unemployed and I still don't see how I'm going to find a job. Okay, I admit it. I have been concentrating just on finding job openings and I'm starting to see some real problems with that. Nobody knows where to find openings. Nobody has any. And when one pops up, everybody fights over it. But what else am I supposed to do?"

"Jessie," I asked, "you see the importance of talking to Decision Makers who don't have openings, right?"

"No, not for me," she said. "It's like you said in the book, they always hire their friends and relatives. I don't have any friends or relatives who are Decision Makers."

"Yes, you do," Ben said. "What about Kate, George, and Harry?"

"Oh c'mon, Ben," Jessie said. "Two of them are all the way across the country, and George only hires computer programmers."

I stepped back in. "So you know three Decision Makers, but they're not the right ones?"

"Yes. That's right. I just know those three. I don't know any real big shots."

"You don't need to," I said, "Remember that 75 percent? The ones who find jobs by talking to Decision Makers before there are openings? They're ordinary people. They talk to other ordinary people. Job hunters don't need to know big shots. They just find a way to connect with the Decision Maker. Usually they talk to someone else who works in the same place—a guy who knows a guy—and that person introduces them."

"And how do they find someone else who works in the same place?" Jessie asked.

Ben jumped back in. "Jessie, you already know at least six people who work inside logical Target Companies. Two of them are even in the right departments."

"Why don't you leave me alone, Ben, about who I supposedly know? And what's a Target Company? Have you read the whole daggone book?" Jessie was starting to raise her voice again.

"There's a bit on target organizations in Chapter 4," I said, "and there's more in Chapter 7. But Ben is right about one thing. You already know enough people. You just need to figure out which ones to talk to and what to ask them. And, Jessie, you are absolutely right that running around and asking everybody about job openings is a waste of time."

"See that, Ben?" Jessie said, "The Big Expert says I'm absolutely right. So I should go ahead and read the rest of the chapter on Project Plan, Orville?"

"Ah," I said, "now I see … you've been reading ahead a bit, too, young lady."

"Yes," said Jessie, "but I don't brag about it."

"Don't worry about Decision Makers yet," I said. "How you get to talk to them will get a lot clearer as we go on. If you see the importance of talking to Decision Makers before they have openings, you're doing very well."

"See that, Ben?" She said. "I'm doing very well. I still don't have a job, but I'm doing well. Very well. I have some more reading to do. Let's go."

She took the book out of Ben's hand as they left.

I went back to my writing.

The Project Plan

1 **Professional Objective**
What kind of work do you want to do?

2 **Target Market**
Which organizations do you want to work for?
Defined by: **Geographic location, Industry or type of organization, Size** (annual revenue or number of employees)

3 **Core Message**
What will you say about yourself to convince Decision Makers in your Target Market that you can do the work in your Professional Objective?

CHAPTER FIVE

Your Project Plan

Some of the people I work with want to be self-employed, to have their own business or professional practice. One of those was Darryl, a computer programming whiz. He always admired his Uncle Jake, a medical doctor. From the time he was a child—and all through college—Darryl had often visited Uncle Jake's office and helped the office staff however he could.

When he graduated from college, Darryl got a job as a programmer with a big computer company. But he didn't forget his Uncle Jake. In his spare time Darryl wrote some new doctor's office software. Darryl's program automatically did everything doctor's offices need—tracked patient care, created bills, dealt with health insurance—everything. His Uncle Jake tested it, and Darryl kept working on it until Jake said it was better than anything you could buy anywhere.

Right around that time, Darryl's employer was bought by an even bigger company, and Darryl, along with 2,499 other people, was laid off. Rather than find a new job, Darryl decided to try to sell the software. He printed up some flyers that said, "Medical Software. Call Darryl. 555-5555." He put them on every windshield of every car at the nearest mall. Then he waited for a response.

But only three doctors ever went to that mall. On the day Darryl was passing out flyers, no doctors went near the place. No one ever called the phone number on the flyer.

What Darryl did is a lot like what some people do in job search. They print a flyer called a resumé. They mail it or e-mail it to people. Then they wait.

No one calls.

What Darryl and the job hunter both need is a better plan—a well-thought-out plan based on how things really work. In Darryl's case it would be what businesspeople call a marketing plan. In the job search project, it's called a Project Plan. Both are logical ways of planning things before you get started.

Darryl's marketing plan needs to label the product he is offering (billing, insurance, and patient record software) and the Target Market most likely to need that product (doctors working in offices). Then he needs to think about his Core Message. What is the best way to describe that product to that Target Market? Maybe it would be something like:

Put our new Physician's Office Assistant to work.
New doctor-tested software does billing,
insurance, and patient records—
All 65 percent faster than other software.

Then he needs to find the best way to get his message to all the doctors in his Target Market. He would find more doctors at a medical convention than a shopping mall. But why wouldn't he start with his Uncle Jake's doctor friends?

The Project Plan does the same three things for a job search that a marketing plan does for a business. The Project Plan identifies:

1. Your Professional Objective: What you're offering, the kind of work that you can do for an employer.
2. Your Target Market: Which employers might need to have that kind of work done.
3. Your Core Message: The best message to communicate to that particular group about how effective you are in that kind of work.

After we discuss those three things, I'll be showing you some very effective ways to get your communications to your Target Market. You may not have an Uncle Jake for a starting point, but there are plenty of other ways to do it.

I also want you to know that you do not need to have your Project Plan completely figured out before you start a search. You just need to get started thinking about the three parts of it. Your plan will improve as you conduct your search. So if you're not clear on all parts of the Project Plan as you read this chapter, don't worry. You don't need to be. You'll learn more as you continue to read. And even more by asking the right questions as you work on your search.

You'll notice that in this and some other parts of the book, I've borrowed some ideas from marketing because they have proven useful to thousands of people in search. I hesitated about including this marketing language because I don't want you to think you have to be a businessperson to succeed in search. Or that you need to be a marketing expert. You don't need to be either.

However, I do think you should professionalize your search with some marketing-style thinking and planning. My goal here is simple: to help you find ways to be smart about how you handle your search—whether you aspire to being a great marketer or not.

Let's continue by looking at each of the three parts of the Project Plan, starting with the Professional Objective.

Your Professional Objective Answers the Question:

What kind of work do you want to do?

Your Professional Objective defines what kind of work you want to do. It's the goal of your search project, the kind of job you want to find. It's called "professional" because it names your profession, whether that is customer relations, human resources, administrative assistant, senior management, or anything else.

Remember, this is NOT a personal objective, such as, "I want a secure, high-paying job in a dynamic growing organization." By naming your profession or general field, you are stating a professional objective. This also tells employers what you have to offer them, just as Darryl named his product so doctors could better see what it can do for them.

Sometimes a Professional Objective is a job title. For example, the titles "Computer Programmer," "Accountant," and "Administrative Assistant" all describe jobs that exist in a wide range of industries. Those titles represent a very large number of jobs and also name a profession. So in these cases the Professional Objective could simply be a job title.

For most of us, though, the objective is less precise, describing a cluster of possible job titles. The Professional Objective, "marketing management," for instance, includes dozens of possible job titles in product management, marketing, and even advertising. "Customer relations" also covers a range of titles. You will find more examples in Chapter 6, "Choosing Your Next Job."

What Your Professional Objective Does for You

Focuses your search.

Makes you a stronger candidate.

Helps you find a job where you will do well and be happy.

Gives you a better resumé.

The clearer you are about your Professional Objective, the easier it is to conduct a good search, because you are describing what you're looking for. When you go to the mall to look for a new pair of shoes, the better you can describe what you want, the easier it is to find them. Do you want men's or women's shoes? For work, play, or dressing up? What color?

If you don't know what you're looking for, you don't know where to look and won't know when you have found it. In job search and shoes, if you can describe what you want, people can help you find it.

I often hear unemployed people say they don't want to "limit their options" by picking a single objective. Employed people usually know better; they do not want just anything. They do want to limit their options to jobs that are clearly better than their current one.

In the end, everyone should limit their options to a cluster of jobs they like—and can convince people they can do. Your Professional Objective focuses your search on the best choices for you. Chapter 9, "How Many Fish Are in That Pond?" will help you be sure you don't narrow your options too much.

A Clear Message for Decision Makers— and Others

If you don't clearly say what kind of job you want, you're asking the employers to figure it out for you. But why would they bother? When you focus on a Professional Objective, you also tell Decision Makers the general area in which you can help them. It's like Darryl saying, "I have some great doctor's office software."

When you are clear about the work you're seeking, you also become a more attractive candidate. You are someone who knows what he or she wants, who is actually interested in a certain kind of work—not just another person looking for a job.

In the course of your search, you will be talking to a lot of people— Decision Makers, recruiters, HR professionals, and a wide range of other contacts. You need to be able to tell all of them—including those who know nothing about your line of work—what kind of work you're looking for. When you use a Professional Objective, you are also telling them what kind of services you have to offer. To make it easy for the people you talk to, you should be able to describe your Professional Objective in one sentence or less. You'll find some examples in the next chapter.

FOCUS ON THE BEST JOBS FOR YOU

There are hundreds of thousands of different jobs out there. You are not qualified for most of them. You would probably hate a lot of them. Your Professional Objective describes a logical cluster of jobs you would do well and enjoy doing. By focusing on those, you stand a much better chance of finding work you will really like. And a better chance of finding work more quickly.

A BETTER RESUMÉ

Finally, your Professional Objective is the key to writing a good resumé. You can't tell if a resumé is good if you don't know what kind of work its owner is seeking. What you need to say to get a job as an HR director is completely different from what you need to say to get a job in marketing, accounting, or nursing. Everything in your resumé needs to support the Professional Objective, to convince people that you can do that particular kind of work well.

When writing your resumé, keep your Professional Objective in front of you. With every sentence you write, ask yourself, "Would this help convince the Decision Maker that I can do that particular kind of work well?" If so, include it. If not, leave it out or downplay it. Even a Professional Objective that is not yet sharply focused is very helpful in resumé writing.

Target Market

Once you have even a fuzzy Professional Objective, you should begin to think about your Target Market. You may find that as you think about the two of them together, they both get clearer. When you start talking to people about both, they will get even clearer. So let's move on to Target Market, the second part of your Project Plan, and start putting that together with your objective.

Your Target Market

Answers the Questions:
Which organizations do you most want to work for?
Who hires people to do the kind of work you want to do?
It becomes a Target List of actual employers.

Along with what kind of work you want, you need to think about where you want to work. Business? Government? Not-for-profit? Large? Small? Manufacturing? Food service? Foundations? Health care? Education? Financial services? This is the part of your Project Plan called your "Target Market."

The term Target Market is borrowed from the business discipline of marketing. There are certain organizations that will buy—or you could say lease—your services. There are others that will not. Banks don't usually hire nurses. High schools don't hire a lot of salespeople.

Just as Darryl knew that doctors' offices were his most likely software buyers, you need to determine which organizations are your best potential buyers, so you can actually list them. A marketing professional might call this defining the demographics of your customers, or defining your Target Market.

Your Target Market in job search is defined partly by where the work is and partly by what you want. You need to come at it two ways: What organizations do you like the best? And: Which organizations might need someone with your skills and abilities? While you must consider both of these, what you want is more important. Being in a job you like and an organization you like is the key to satisfying and rewarding work. And the key to getting ahead.

How To Define Your Target Market

The geographic location of your targets.
The industry or type of organization you want to join.
The size of the organization you want to join.

Let's look at each of the three ways you define your Target Market.

GEOGRAPHIC LOCATION

Will you pursue all relevant employers in the world? Or are you confining yourself to 20 minutes travel from where you live? Location is determined by personal preference (Where do you want to live and how far will you travel?) and by market demand (Where is the work?). You need to consider both. Personal preference is more important for most people, since most don't want to relocate or have a long commute. But you'll also need to be sure that there are enough potential jobs, and I'll show you how to do that in Chapter 9.

You need to define your geographic preferences so they can be drawn on a map, and it might be a good idea to actually do that. Common ways of doing this are by country, state, province, county, city limits, and postal codes. It needs to be precisely defined so you can take the next step: actually creating a Target List, which I'll tell you about in Chapter 7, "Your Target List."

INDUSTRY OR TYPE OF ORGANIZATION

In what industry would you like to work? Again, this is partly a matter of personal preference. But your industry choices can also be determined by your Professional Objective. For instance, someone with an objective of "metallurgist" will probably target metals and metal products industries. Someone with an objective of "law enforcement" might target law enforcement agencies of all kinds, private security companies, and organizations with their own security forces.

If your Professional Objective were "bookkeeping and office administration" or for that matter, "senior financial manager," you would have a very wide range of industry choices, since nearly all organizations include people with those skills. You might be seen as a stronger candidate in certain industries because of your past experience.

Even someone with highly transferable skills, like an accountant, may be seen as a better candidate in the industry where they have worked. An accountant with 15 years of experience in the chemical industry will probably have more appeal in that industry than others. That accountant can surely succeed in many industries and should probably consider more than one. However, the chemical industry might find them particularly attractive.

SIZE OF ORGANIZATION

Your third decision is the size of the employer you want to work for. Size is usually defined by annual revenue (or budget) or by the number of employees. These are useful measures because databases and directories typically use them.

You'll need to use some kind of numerical measure when you talk to people, since everyone has a different idea of what "medium-sized" is. An accurate definition of size also tells you exactly which organizations to put on your Target List—and which to leave off. You should use whatever numerical measurements of size make sense for your search.

For a Professional Objective like "outside salesperson," the revenue number, how much the company sells each year, is probably more relevant. For an objective like "Human Resources management," the number of employees is more relevant. Other measures are sometimes used. Hospitals, for example, may go by number of beds, and financial institutions by assets under management.

The employer's size can be a critical factor in your planning. Below a certain size, for instance, a company will not have a staff attorney or a director of human resources. A company with 10 employees may have only one administrative assistant position, while a company of 1,000 could have dozens. Salary is also a factor. A chief financial officer is not likely to make $150,000 a year in a company with $1 million in annual revenue, but could in a larger one.

Size is also a matter of personal preference. You might be happier working in a job in a large organization with a lot of coworkers and a nice big building. Or maybe you would prefer a small organization, where you know everyone and everyone is more involved in everything. Or maybe the employer's size doesn't matter to you at all.

A TARGET LIST OF POTENTIAL EMPLOYERS

All of that might sound like a lot of work, but it really isn't. It's just a way of thinking about things. Those Target Market parameters —geographic location, industry, and size—are the key to making a Target List of potential employers, which is a huge advantage in a search. You can enter those three in a database and it will produce a Target List for you. You can do the same thing using printed directories in a library—both databases and directories use the same definitions of geography, industry, and size. Either way, you will get a good look at your personal job market. And a list of names of actual employers.

That's why I'm asking you to define those three factors. I'll give you the details on how to convert them to a Target List in Chapter 7, "Your Target List." For now, let's look at the benefits of defining your Target Market and having a Target List.

What Your Target Market Does for You

Makes sure your search includes all worthwhile employers.
Gives you a tool to organize your efforts.
Makes sure that your personal job market is big enough.
Prepares you for a proactive search, covering all three hiring scenarios.

Once they've written a resumé, many people take a passive approach to job hunting, waiting and hoping for the right employer to place the right ad in the paper or on the Internet. This, of course, limits them to Scenario 1, the Applicant Pool, and about 25 percent of the job market. If you want to get beyond waiting and hoping and take an active approach, the first step is defining your Target Market and creating a Target List of the employers in it. This proactive approach leaves much less to chance. It ensures that you leave no stone unturned.

I want to remind you again that you are NOT simply going to send resumés to the employers on your Target List. We'll be looking at much more effective search techniques. But before you use any search techniques, it helps to know which Target Market you're going to pursue.

Making a Target List of employers in your Target Market is also a way of prioritizing your efforts in the search. You collect information on your targeted employers and use that to refine your Target List, throwing out employers you don't like and deciding which are the best ones for you. Each week, you work on pursuing the best employers on your Target List.

As you will see in Chapter 9, "How Many Fish Are in That Pond?" working on your Target Market early in your search allows you to do a Reality Check on your Project Plan. Some job hunters stall out simply because they are focused on a Target Market that is too small. Preparing a Target List is a way to ensure that you're pursuing a market with plenty of potential jobs in it—and covering the Known Candidate and Created Position scenarios as well as the Applicant Pool.

What Your Target List Does for You

**Opens the door to the Known Candidate
and Created Position scenarios.**

Helps you focus your efforts.

Increases your chances of finding a great employer.

Remember the Known Candidate scenario in the last chapter? The one where you reduce competition by becoming known to the Decision Maker before they have a job opening? The one that encompasses about 75 percent of all hiring?

Your Target List is the key to becoming a known candidate, since it is how you select the organizations in your Target Market that are best for you. Your Target list also opens the door to the Created Position scenario. In both cases, you decide which group of organizations you want to proactively pursue. Then you collect the information you need to prioritize the organizations you have listed.

Once you have a Target List, your job every week is to pursue the top organizations on that list. And to collect more information on targets so you can continue to refine and better prioritize the list. As you will see, the Target List itself is a tool that will help you do both of these.

When talking to friends and acquaintances in job search, showing them your Target List is usually more important than showing them your resumé. It leads to conversations that are both comfortable and productive. It produces useful information. It's the first step on the path to making yourself known to the right Decision Makers.

Because you are always focusing your proactive efforts on the best targets on your list, you have a better chance of ending up at an organization you truly like. When you just pursue announced openings, your choices are limited to those organizations that are advertising this week.

A TARGET LIST IS ESSENTIAL

Your Target List is just as important as your resumé. Without a Target List, your search will be unfocused and disorganized, leaving too much to chance. With a Target List, you are constantly focused on the best employers and proactively pursuing the next available opening in that group of organizations.

Once you have an idea who your targeted organizations are, you are ready to think about how to talk to them. This is your Core Message, the third and last part of your Project Plan.

Your Core Message

Answers the Questions:

What will you say about yourself to Decision Makers in your Target Market?

How will you describe yourself in one minute?

Provides evidence that you can do the work defined by your Professional Objective.

Your Core Message is how you will convince employers on your Target List that you are qualified for the work defined by your Professional Objective. The question here is: "What can you honestly say about yourself that will convince Decision Makers in your Target Market that you are a good candidate for the objective you are pursuing?"

As soon as you start thinking this way, you do a better job of talking about yourself. When you consider your Professional Objective, you know what to emphasize and what to leave out. When you consider the particular group of Decision Makers in a particular Target Market, you can make good guesses on what they will think is important.

YOUR QUALIFICATIONS AND HOW YOU TALK ABOUT THEM

Of course, you need to have some of the expected qualifications for your Professional Objective. But having all of them is not usually necessary. Having some that are relevant but not usually expected is also a plus.

Time and again I talk to people who tell me their qualifications are weak. I hear this from senior managers and recent graduates alike. But it always turns out that they have many more qualifications than they thought. They have skills gained from life as well as work experience.

And so do you. You do have qualifications, and you need to pick the most relevant ones to talk about. And it's most important that you know how you talk about your qualifications. Can you name all of them? Many people are not aware of all the skills they've picked up over the years. Do you know which of your skills your Target Market is most interested in?

For most people in search, this takes some thought. At the outset, sometimes they cannot even name their key qualifications, much less discuss them. They literally do not know how good they are.

Once you can name all of your qualifications, the next step is to organize them into a brief presentation designed to convince the particular group of Decision Makers you have targeted. This is why it's so important to know who those Decision Makers are.

Explaining your qualifications in an hour to a sympathetic and skilled interviewer is easier than doing that in two minutes with a Decision Maker who is not trained in interviewing and has no current opening. Or doing it in one minute.

Any of these may be required in a search. The first step in preparing for all of them is getting clear on the Professional Objective and Target Market. Then you will more easily see what to include in your Core Message.

What Your Core Message Does for You

Tells you what to include in your resumé.
Lays the foundation for interview success.
Creates powerful consistent communication.

One of the fascinating things about job search is that many employers will make decisions about you based only on information they get from you. They read the resumé that you wrote. They talk to you on the phone once or twice. They meet with you in a one-hour interview. Then, based on what you told them, they make a decision.

Many employers these days do not check references, or do not check them until after they hire you. If they hear about you from someone else, that person may just be repeating some of the positive things you told them. You are often the number one source of the employer's information about you.

Since you have something between 18 and 80 years of life experience behind you, there is a lot you could say about yourself. But you probably have only one hour and two pages of a resumé to say it. So you need to make some choices. That's what a Core Message is all about.

Your Core Message ensures that you have a good resumé, because you have thought about who the targeted readers are and what they want in employees. Exactly the same kind of thinking will make you effective in interviewing. In fact, the main points on your resumé are likely to be some of the main points you make in a different way in most of your interviews. People who have thought through a Project Plan do better in resumé writing and interviewing.

A CONSISTENT POWERFUL MESSAGE

In a job search, you will talk about yourself again and again to many different people. In doing that, you'll repeat yourself. A Core Message is how you make sure that what you're repeating again and again is the best possible message about how good you are at doing the work in your Professional Objective.

Sometimes I see people go the other way, repeating again and again to everyone who will listen how difficult unemployment is. Or how much they dislike their last employer for having a downsizing. This kind of talk damages their search. Why would anyone want to hire that poor victim? Or recommend them to a Decision Maker?

When you constantly maintain a positive focus on your main selling points, people get the message—and begin to repeat it to others, including Decision Makers. It's the same thing that businesses do in advertising. Volvo cars are an example. They have been telling us for years how safe Volvos are. Ask someone about safe cars and they'll probably mention Volvo. Ask them about Volvos and they'll probably mention safety.

You won't be spending millions on advertising like Volvo does, and your message will be a little more complicated. But a Core Message gives you a simple message about yourself and how good you are at a particular kind of work. Repeating that message to a lot of people is a powerful step toward new employment.

Using Your Project Plan

An effective job search uses some ideas from marketing. The marketing plan and Project Plan both generate focused effective activities. The marketer and the job seeker each have something valuable to offer.

Each figures out who might have use for it (the Target Market), makes a Target List of potential buyers (Decision Makers), and prepares a presentation (the Core Message used in resumés and interviews). Both the marketer and the job seeker then let the right people know what a great offering they have.

Sooner or later one of these Decision Makers has a need, requests more information, and then purchases the product (hires you). But what you're doing is also completely different from marketing. Marketers don't care who they sell to. You do. You will work only for an organization you like. Marketers want to sell thousands or even millions of things every year. You only need one employer.

In job search, the Project Plan consists of a Professional Objective, a Target Market (defined by geographic location, industry, or type of organization and size), and a Core Message.

If you do not think through each of these three pieces, or if they do not fit together, your search project will go more slowly. If you do think them through, you not only save time, you can achieve better results. Once again, you don't need to have everything completely figured out. Just get started thinking about them. And discussing them with friends.

The next three chapters elaborate on each of the three parts of the Project Plan, and how to best think them through and put them together. If you're already clear on one (or more) parts of your Project Plan, you may not need to read that chapter as carefully.

The Project Plan is a way of clearly defining what success looks like and creating a road map to get there. After all, you don't want just any job, and you're not qualified for all of them anyway. You don't want just any employer, you want a place you like with people you like.

No one but you can answer the three questions in the Project Plan: What kind of work do you want? What kind of organization do you want? And what will you say to Decision Makers? These questions are about who you are and what you want in your work life. The clearer your answers to them, the more likely you are to have a happy and successful work life.

In fact, I've heard it said by some very respectable philosophers that if you're clear on what you desire and continue to desire it, you'll definitely get it. Since that might actually be a law of the universe, we'll spend the next three chapters on the three parts of your Project Plan to make sure that what you get is exactly what you want.

ORVILLE'S JOURNAL

BEN AND I DISCUSS THE PROJECT PLAN, IGNORING JESSIE MORE THAN WE SHOULD HAVE

Jessie and Ben were seated comfortably on their living room sofa. They had invited me for coffee and to discuss Chapter 5. I can do without coffee, but I like cookies. Jessie had put some on the table next to my rocking chair.

"Orville, come on, tell me. Why are you making it so complicated?" Jessie asked. "Why do I have to do all this Project Plan stuff? I don't want a project. I just want a job. I'll mail some resumés and get one."

"Yes," said Ben before I could answer, "like you've been doing for three months now. Mailing resumés. What has it gotten you? No interviews. No job."

I finished a cookie and reached for another. "How many resumés have you mailed?"

"In the whole three months?" Jessie asked.

"Yes."

"Oh, gosh, a lot. An awful lot. I guess 50 or 100 a month."

"Well, that's 150 to 300 altogether," I said. "That sounds like a lot, but it usually takes more than that."

"More!" Jessie was shocked. "More than 300?"

"Yes," I said. "I'm sorry, but mailing resumés to strangers is just not a very good search technique. Mailings usually need to be much larger than 300."

"MUCH larger?"

"Yes," I replied, "that's one reason why they're not such a great way to go.

"But the real point here is that a Project Plan always plays a big role, even in a resumé mailing. You need to mail them to the right Target Market. You want the message in the resumé and cover letter directed to the right Decision Makers, to convince them you can do the work in your Professional Objective."

"I hate you, Orville. You think you're so smart. You're such a snotty know-it-all."

"Now, dear ... " Ben said.

"Don't 'now dear' me, Ben. Whose side are you on?"

"It's okay," I said. "People in job search get upset. It's not always what you'd call a fun job."

"You know, hon," Ben said, "Orville's just doing his job. "He's trying to help you get your search organized. I think that makes sense. In any project, you need to get it organized. You need to figure it out."

"That's true," I said. "Too many people in job search just list out their past jobs on a resumé. Then they expect the employer to figure it out. But the employer won't do that. If they want a bookkeeper, they want someone who walks in and says, 'I'm a great bookkeeper. I love bookkeeping.' Or engineering or management or whatever they're looking for."

"That's right," said Ben, "and the job hunter better know what the supervisor in the bookkeeping department thinks is important. Know it and show it. That's Core Message, right?"

"Right," I replied, "and the targeting is important too. Nurses usually consider hospitals and medical practices, but do they consider other health organizations? Government agencies? Insurance companies or the big drug companies?"

"Yeah, and this Target List thing makes good sense too," Ben said. "With a Target List, you would know what to concentrate on. Where to spend your time. Who to talk to."

"Well, aren't the two of you both big bad experts?" asked Jessie. It was then, way too late, that I realized we had forgotten the most important person in this conversation. And that she had moved the cookies out of my reach.

"Ben the Big Expert. Orville the Big Expert. Everybody knows what I should do in my job search but me. So if I'd spent the last three months making a Project Plan instead of mailing resumés, I'd be better off, right?" asked Jessie.

"That's not fair to Orville," shot Ben. "He's just trying to help. He never said to spend three months on a Project Plan. He just said make one."

"Okay, Ben. You're right," said Jessie. "But Orville, you're basically telling me I wasted my time mailing resumés, aren't you?"

"Jessie, you don't need me to tell you if it worked or not," I replied. "Sometimes it does. What you sent out could still bring you an interview. But direct mail takes very large numbers. Other techniques are usually more effective."

"Well, we all know it didn't work this time," Jessie said. "And, Orville, you're right about something else too."

"What's that?" I asked. I wasn't used to being right in these conversations. Or to hearing Jessie say that Ben was right about anything. Ever.

"I haven't been focused," she continued. "Not on the kind of work I want and certainly not on my Target Market or whatever you call it. I never thought about either one, not once. But now I'm thinking about both of them. And I have some new ideas about targets—and about my search."

"That's great," I said. "What are they?"

Jessie looked me straight in the eye. "I'll tell you later," she said, heading out to the kitchen. She left, I might add, with the rest of the cookies.

But she was smiling now. I suspected that she was about to start a much more effective search.

Your Professional Objective

What kind of work
do you want to do?

CHAPTER SIX

Choosing Your Next Job

Training career consultants has been part of my job for many years. I have taught classes for hundreds of career professionals in a wide range of subjects. When I first started doing it, I was nervous. Did I know enough to teach a class for professionals in the field? I had many years of experience, but some of them had master's degrees and Ph.D.s as well as experience.

But I quickly confirmed what I already knew: Career consultants are a friendly and helpful group of people. Being in a room full of them is easy and fun. If someone with a Ph.D. knew more than I did about a particular topic, they helped teach that part, benefiting me as well as the class. Over the years, I may have learned more by teaching career consulting than I learned by doing it.

Career consulting includes two areas: career counseling and job search coaching. The first involves working with clients on personal decisions relating to career choices. It's about who you are as a person and how that fits with what you do in your work life. It's an introspective process. The counselor's job is to help the client look inside to find subjective answers to personal questions about work.

The second area, job search coaching, is about making things happen in the real world. It is about performance, project management, and getting the job done. Whether the client is seeking work in business, not-for-profits, academia, or government, the coach's job always uses some ideas from marketing. The client needs to be practical and make objective decisions about the best ways to operate in the job market.

As you can see, career counseling and job search coaching are quite different. They use different skills sets. A career consultant needs to have a wide range of skills and unusual personal maturity to be good at both.

As different as they are—the subjective/personal and objective/practical—they come together in a job search. You need to look for work that fits who you are as a person. But the choice must also be practical, so you can realistically expect to find that work and earn enough money doing it. And you certainly need to be practical and objective about conducting your search.

This chapter is about the subjective part. Choosing your next job is an important decision about your life. While getting advice on how to do that can be useful, in the end you will make the decision by yourself and for yourself. Choosing what kind of work you want to do is a very personal decision.

As a career counselor, I have often had the experience of asking the central question about Professional Objective—What kind of work do you want?—only to have my client shrug and reply, "I have no idea."

I remember one man in particular who gave this answer. His name was Adam, and he had about 15 years of work experience. When I asked what kind of work he wanted now, he replied, "I don't know. I don't have a clue." He added that he wanted to take aptitude tests. He said that the only thing he was sure of was that he would never take a job like his last one again. He hated it, he said. He hated everything about it.

I explained that aptitude testing was not usually helpful for someone with as much professional experience as he had. After he agreed that we could start by just talking about it for a while, I asked him a series of questions. Because I knew he was coming from a series of well-paying white collar professional jobs, I was pretty sure I already knew the answers to most of them. But I wanted to illustrate something for him. Here are the questions I asked and how he responded:

Would you like to work outdoors?
No. Are you kidding? In the winter? In the rain? No way.

Would you like to work with your hands?
No. I have a college degree in philosophy. I like to use my mind.

How about something scientifically oriented?
No. I never liked science much. I flunked chemistry in college.

How about something involving analytical thinking?
Yes. I always liked that. I've done it in every job I ever had. It was why I was successful in all of my last three jobs.

At this point Adam started laughing. "I get it," he said. "When I told you that I didn't have a clue, that was baloney. I do have clues. Lots of them. I just haven't started putting them together. I don't need aptitude testing. I need to think some more. And ask the logical questions to narrow it down."

As it turned out, he didn't hate everything about his last job. Only some things. He had a bad year with the wrong boss on the wrong projects. But even then, there were some things he liked and wanted to continue doing—if he could do them in a slightly different job with a very different boss in a different organization.

HOW TO BE YOUR OWN CAREER COUNSELOR

I thought a lot about how to write this chapter, because career counseling is usually a dialogue between the counselor and client, like the one I just illustrated. But it is also an internal dialogue, a conversation in your mind. It is entirely possible to ask yourself the questions.

So what I'm going to do in this chapter is teach you how to be your own career counselor. I have condensed what I teach career professionals to one chapter. I'll suggest a way to organize your thinking and tell you the most important questions to ask. As you work on it, you will probably find it useful to discuss your thinking on career decisions with other people.

While your friends and relatives may not be the very best professional career counselors, their hourly fee for talking to you is probably much lower too. If reading this chapter, thinking it over, and talking to people aren't enough to get you to a good decision on Professional Objective, there are some additional suggestions at the end of the chapter.

NO CHANGE, SMALL CHANGE, BIG CHANGE

Perhaps you may already know exactly what kind of work you want.

Sometimes the decision is easy. If you have experience in a certain kind of work, enjoy it, and there are no major obstacles to continuing in the field, by all means look for a similar new job. If this describes you, you should still take a quick look at this chapter to be sure you're making the right decision on your Professional Objective. But you may not need to do all of the things suggested here.

Some people decide to look for a different kind of work because the work they've done in the past is no longer satisfactory to them. Some may want only minor changes that can easily be included in their Professional Objective or Target Market.

Others want a large change. Since this could require more search time and effort, unemployed people may be smarter to make a big change in several smaller steps. For example, if you wanted to change to a completely new job title, you might decide to go for your old job title in an organization that had both the old and new titles. Then, after you got established, you could transfer to the new job title. Another possibility is to find a new job that combines elements of the new and old job titles so that you are a step closer to your goal.

Or you may simply make the leap. When people succeed in making large career changes in one big leap, it is often because the Decision Maker knows them personally or has heard of them from a trusted source.

This definitely applies to the biggest change of all: graduating from any kind of school and starting your first "real" job. If you're in this category, I hope that you will talk to your parents, aunts, uncles, and other older relatives about your job search. They are likely to be in the same age bracket as your next boss (or even your next boss's boss)—and may even have met that person.

UNHAPPY AT WORK?

If you're thinking about finding a new job because you are unhappy in your current job, please think very carefully before making a move. That old saying about not throwing the baby out with the bathwater definitely applies here. Get some help examining your work situation if you need it.

And ask yourself a lot of questions. What is the cause of your unhappiness? Is it what you do on a day-to-day basis? Is it your relationship with your boss or others on the job? Or is it your department or the whole organization you don't like? Is it a problem with working conditions? Have things changed since you took the job? If so, what? The organization? You?

If you are employed and something's not working, I hope you will thoroughly explore ways to improve things in your current organization before deciding to look elsewhere. If it's people problems, can they be mended? Is a transfer possible? If so, what kind of work in what department would you prefer? If the issue is advancement, what do you want to advance to? Looking for work inside an organization can be similar to looking outside, in that you need to ask some of the same questions.

Sometimes a bad work situation can be turned into a good one by talking to the right people in the right way—which is never about complaining and always about offering solutions that benefit everyone, not just you.

Whether you are looking for new opportunities with your current employer or in the general job market, an essential starting point is your Professional Objective—the kind of work you want to do next. Your Professional Objective is a very brief statement of the kind of work you're looking for right now. In writing it, you will think about what you do *not* want as well as what you *do* want in your work. Here is the first step:

Three Key Areas in Creating Your Professional Objective

Your interests: What you like to do.
Your skills: What you are good at doing.
Your values: What's important to you in life.

Career counselors helping people work on a Professional Objective typically start by examining three basic areas: interests, skills, and values. You could say that these three are at the heart of Career Counseling 101. Let's take a look at each.

INTERESTS

Many career counselors these days talk about having a "passion" for a certain kind of work. People also talk about loving your work. There is even a book called *Do What You Love, the Money Will Follow*. Personally, I think it's great when people love their work or experience their work as play or feel passionate about it. But while those are great when they happen, I don't think that any of them are *necessary*. Some people will always have their greatest loves and passions outside of the workplace.

So I don't think you need to have a passionate attraction to a particular kind of work, but I do believe that it's important to find work that interests you. After all, the opposite of interest is disinterested, bored, or worse. So I think it would be good if your feelings toward the work you're looking for were somewhere between interest and passion.

You might ask yourself: What kind of work engages me? What kind of work are my heart and mind both attracted to? Interests are a good starting point for developing a Professional Objective for your search because you are likely to do better at work that interests you. For a recent graduate with little experience, interest is central.

You are also a stronger candidate when you show a genuine interest in a particular kind of work. People with a strong interest will develop skills more quickly. People with strong skills but no interest are not very good employees.

WHAT IF YOU'RE NOT SURE WHAT WORK INTERESTS YOU?

Sometimes people are very sure that they need an income, but not so sure what kind of work would interest them most. This can be because they don't know a lot about what the possibilities are. Or it can be simply because they haven't thought much about it.

When you are looking for new work is a great time to think about what interests you. You have an opportunity to get your work better aligned with who you are as a person.

Career counselors sometimes use interest inventories to help you focus more clearly on what does and does not interest you in your work life. These formal questionnaires commonly ask a long series of multiple-choice questions. The best of them usually cannot be found on the Internet—at least not for free—because you need a trained professional to help you understand the results.

A simpler and less expensive approach is to ask yourself a series of questions, just as I did with Adam. Later in this chapter you'll find a list of "Either/Or" categories of the kind I used with him. What you are NOT interested in is just as important as what you are interested in. It's all about narrowing it down.

If you have work experience, you can (and should) go through it and ask: What did I really enjoy doing, and what did I dislike? Review each and every work experience you have ever had—full- or part-time, paid or unpaid, even work projects in school or at home—and list what you liked best and least about each. Then combine the lists into a master list.

These two lists are a great indication of your interests. The "dislikes" tell you where your interests are not; what to avoid in future work. The "likes" create a picture of your interests. This is a great exercise because it helps you write a Professional Objective for a next job that will have more of what you like and less of what you dislike. Your interests have an effect on your choice of Target Market or where you will work, as well as on what you'll do.

SKILLS

Once you have established what interests you in work, you should look at your skills. While you don't need to have all of the expected skills to get the job that truly interests you, it helps if you have some of them. You may also be more interested in using some of your skills than others.

Skills are those things you have practiced and can now do well. They are the product of experience. Employers ask about past job titles and experience because it's an easy way to see what skills you might have. You may have picked up exactly the right skills in the "wrong" job titles. If so, you will need to work a bit harder to show the employer that you have them.

You may have acquired your skills through formal work experience, experience in educational projects, or life experience. You may have found it easy to build certain skills because you were born with a related talent. Along with your skills, you've probably developed areas of specialized knowledge—which is also part of your skill package.

Virtually every client I have ever worked with has initially understated their skills. This is true of students looking for their first job and also of high-level executives and administrators. I believe that the reason is simple: We all acquire most of our skills on the job, rather than in school. With on-the-job learning, there is no instructor to tell you what you're learning and how well you're learning it.

In school, you get a transcript of all your courses, so listing exactly what you learned there is easy. On the job, you learn even more, but you may not notice how much you learned or have names for the skills you acquired.

A SKILLS INVENTORY CAN HELP ANYONE IN SEARCH

An important early step in job search is therefore creating an inventory of your skills. Along with your interests, this skills list will help you select a Professional Objective. Even if you already know what kind of work you want, a skills inventory will help you write a better resumé. It will also help you interview more effectively, because it will remind you to talk about *all* of your relevant skills.

A good way to do a skills inventory is to list out your accomplishments, the contributions you made in each job, large and small, and analyze them to see what skills they required. You can include unpaid experience too. Concentrate on the accomplishments you enjoyed doing. First list the contributions, then list the skills you used to accomplish each. Then look to see which skills come up the most often.

Organize the most frequently used skills into three to six logical clusters and give each a name reflecting the entire skill category. Do these categories tie in to jobs you are interested in? Do the skill clusters suggest any other jobs you might be interested in?

Talking to others about your skills can be very useful. If you're using a friend as a career counselor, ask your friend to help you sift through your past experience for skills. Talk through each job you ever had with that person. Tell your friend exactly what you did and have your friend help you list the skills it took to do those things. Cover the routine, day-to-day things you did and also those times when you went above and beyond the job description.

Anyone interviewing for any job needs to be able to talk about their skills (and skill clusters, or competencies). Your Professional Objective defines the group of jobs you want to interview for. In formulating a Professional Objective, you will look for one that fits your skills. You will also adjust how you cluster, label, and discuss your skills to fit your Professional Objective.

If you want more help with this work on skills—or anything else in this chapter—take a look at pages 115 to 116 for some suggestions.

VALUES

Values are your beliefs about what is most and least important in life. You may not talk about them a lot, but you make decisions based on them. You feel uncomfortable when your values are compromised and satisfied when they are fulfilled. Values evolve over the course of a lifetime, changing gradually with age and experience, so it might be worth looking to see if yours have shifted.

Your work should be consistent with your values. So if you value money and advancement, you want work that will satisfy those values. Or if you value service to others, you might be happier in work that satisfies that value. And if you value good health or the environment, you might object to doing work that you thought did harm in these areas.

There are hundreds of things you might value. Examples include challenge, security, leadership, autonomy, personal achievement, using technical expertise, and many, many others. The question here is which three or four areas are *most* important to you. There is some overlap between values and interests.

Value surveys are easier to create and use than interest inventories, and you can find them in career books and on the Internet. But the central question is not difficult: What is important to you in your life in general that carries over into your work life?

If, for example, having honest personal relationships with a wide range of people is particularly important to you, then that is a high value of yours. Do you want to express that value at work, or is expressing it in your personal life sufficient? If you want it at work, you may want to look at jobs that include such relationships with clients or customers. Or at organizations where those relationships with other employees are part of the culture.

Skills, interests, and values are the three most important areas to consider in determining a Professional Objective. But there are three additional factors you may also want to take a look at.

Three More Factors in Creating a Professional Objective

Your personality.

Your long-term career goals and life plan.

Your mission, purpose, or vision.

Career counselors also frequently work with clients in these three areas. Sometimes these three are less important. But sometimes one of them is very important and the key to finding the right kind of work. Let's look at each.

PERSONALITY

While skills are undoubtedly important in the hiring process, it is also true that employers hire people, not skills. In some jobs, your personality is actually more important than your skills. Jobs that involve constantly relating to a wide range of people are an example. After all, it might be easier for an employer to locate a naturally outgoing, friendly, sensitive, extroverted personality than to train someone to be that way when it doesn't come naturally.

In any job, it's important for you to be able to be yourself, not struggling to be a personality you are not. For example, some people are more extroverted and some are more introverted. If you're a natural introvert, you might be happy in introverted jobs, those that require working alone—or in a small group—for long periods, perhaps concentrating on a single activity. If you're a natural extrovert, you might be happier in jobs that include a wide range of activities and relating to a wide range of people.

The same is true of personality tendencies toward analysis, human service, creativity, practicality, and many others. Some jobs are more consistent with one personality preference, some with another. There are psychological "tests"—instruments, actually—designed to sort out and put names on personality traits.

But another way of coming at it is to ask yourself (and your friends) some questions. Have people always said that you are a "salesy" kind of person? That you are detail-oriented? Analytical? A natural leader? Any of these can be an indication of personality traits that might suggest particular kinds of work—and certain kinds of Professional Objectives.

LONG-TERM GOALS

In determining your Professional Objective, you should consider what you want from your work and career in the long term and make sure that your next job is a step in the right direction. In fact, sometimes the best way to work on your Professional Objective is to ask what kind of work you'd most like to be doing in five or 10 years. Then ask what kind of work (and organization) right now would be a step in that direction.

Sometimes I've talked to people who wistfully describe a job they'd like to have in the distant future, if only they could one day get it. Then as we talk more, we discover that they can actually get it right now. And they do. A little long-term thinking is useful for anyone working on a Professional Objective. And you never know how long the "long term" might turn out to be.

In addition to thinking longer term, you may also want to think more broadly—beyond your work, into what you want your life to look like. Sometimes your work sets up a particular lifestyle. Work that requires travel is an example. For some the lifestyle it creates is damaging, far from what they want. For others it opens possibilities for a much more satisfying life. Considering your long-term life plan might also produce clues for what kind of work you want now.

MISSION, PURPOSE, OR VISION

Some career counselors (and some of their clients) always start with this one. Others do not see any value in it at all. The idea here is to start with a picture—an aerial view from 30,000 feet—of how you want your life and work to look. Then you translate that picture into specifics in all areas of life, including work.

Do you think of yourself as having a particular mission or purpose in life, with a particular kind of work playing a role in fulfilling it? Do you like to start with a vision of how your life and work will look at some future date and use that to create immediate goals? If you see your work as a vocation or "calling," you are also in this category.

Some people do not relate to this way of thinking at all. If this way of approaching life is part of who you are, make it part of determining your Professional Objective.

These six—interests, skills, values, personality, long-term goals, and mission/vision—are what I spend the most time on when training new career consultants. Here are some suggestions on how to put them together when you are determining your Professional Objective.

Choose a Professional Objective Based on Your Interests

Then ask:

Do you want it? (Check your values, personality, mission, and long-term plans.)

Can you get it? (Check your skills, knowledge, and experience.)

Of the six factors used in determining Professional Objective, interests are usually the best starting point. I suggest that you let your interests lead the way in making career choices.

Based on your interests, what would be your ideal job? Start without reference to practical constraints. If you had the right education and experience, what jobs would you be enthusiastic about? The jobs, for instance, where you would never watch the clock? After you list these, see how they fit with your values, personality, mission, and long-term objectives. Use those four factors to refine your picture of the ideal job.

CHECK TO SEE IF IT'S PRACTICAL

If none of your ideal jobs are practical right now, what practical options are similar? What real jobs would be stepping-stones toward the ideal jobs? How close can you get to the ideal? What elements of the ideal can be found in other jobs? For example, if medical doctor were on your ideal job list but this is impractical, what elements of that job interest you most? Science? Helping people? Working with the sick? Prestige? Hospital environments? Other than being a medical doctor, how could you attain these?

When you have some ideas that might be practical, check them against your skills. Are your skills and experience sufficient to qualify you for jobs you're interested in? If you're not sure, talk to people who know the field.

CAREER EXPLORATION

If you have limited work experience or you're considering large changes, you should do some career exploration—reading about possible jobs and talking to people who actually do them. Visiting people in your new field in their workplace is a great way to see if you would like that kind of work—and particularly useful for recent (or about-to-be) graduates. For anyone, talking to others is an important part of settling on the right Professional Objective.

In all of this, remember that you have choices—and probably more choices than you think. The first step is to see that you have many choices. Then you need to narrow it down to a workable, practical Professional Objective.

EITHER/OR'S

People at the beginning of their careers and those considering a major change may need to do additional work on formulating a Professional

Either/Or's
WHICH DO YOU PREFER?

Working with people, data, or things?

Alone or with others?

Academic, government, not-for-profit, or business?

Doing a variety of tasks or focusing on a few tasks?

Creative or practical?

Involving analysis and logic or empathy and compassion?

Indoors or outdoors?

Involving decision making or requiring spontaneity?

Physical or mental?

Travel or not?

Team member or solo performer?

Artistic, administrative, or neither?

Social service, "hands on," or neither?

Scientific, business, or neither?

Management or individual contributor?

Objective. Using either/or's can be a useful way of narrowing down your interests and beginning to name and classify them.

One classical career counseling approach starts by asking whether you would prefer to spend your workday interacting with people, handling data, or in "hands on" work, dealing with physical objects. People sometimes have strong preferences in the people/data/things categories, and these preferences can quickly narrow the field of possible jobs.

The above list of either/or categories is commonly used for getting more focused when writing career objectives. They are all written as questions, the kind of questions I asked Adam in the beginning of this chapter. In using them, remember that some of the choices include a "neither" choice, and some could include a "both" choice.

Whether you use these either/or's or work with the six categories discussed in this chapter or both, in the end you will need to write a brief Professional Objective encapsulating your decision.

Your Professional Objective
It should be one sentence or less.
It should not be too broad nor too narrow.

A written Professional Objective is an important search tool. You can use it at the top of your resumé as a headline that immediately tells readers what category of potential employee you are. But whether it heads the resumé or not, the Professional Objective is essential in determining if a resumé is effective. In fact, your resumé is effective only if it helps you get the kind of work described by the Professional Objective. Just as important, your Professional Objective is the starting point for your Project Plan.

Your Professional Objective must be short, clear, and concise. When you're talking to people in the course of your search—friends, recruiters, Decision Makers—you need to let them know exactly what you are looking for. You need to do this briefly. Most recruiters and Decision Makers would expect you to define it in less than 30 seconds. Even your friends should not be expected to listen to a five minute answer to: "What kind of work are you looking for?"

The trick in writing a good objective is: not too narrow, not too broad. Common examples of too broad include, "I'm looking for a job," "I'm looking for something in management," or "I want to work with people."

In most cases, a single job title is too narrow. However, there are some—like accountant, outside sales, programmer, administrative assistant, or nurse—that are well known, used in many (or all) organizations, and account for so many jobs that they are great Professional Objectives.

NAME YOUR PROFESSION

Your Professional Objective should always name your profession. Go back and look at the one- and two-word Professional Objectives in the above paragraph. Each could also be called a profession. If you don't already think of yourself as having a profession, it might be a good idea to do so.

In the twentieth century, only those occupations requiring an extensive formal training—like medical doctor, accountant, nurse, or lawyer—were seen as professions. Now, in the twenty-first century, work is increasingly complex and the definition of "profession" is much broader. Any kind of work associated with a particular well-defined set of skills and body of knowledge can be called a profession. So your Professional Objective always identifies which professional area you want to work in.

When it is not a single job title, a Professional Objective usually describes a cluster of related job titles or uses a broad generic term applicable to many jobs, organizations, and industries. Some examples are:

Human Resources Management
Chemical Engineering
Teaching or Training
Senior Financial Management
Law Enforcement
Manufacturing Operations
Research and Development
Customer Relations
Financial Development
Purchasing
Information Technology Management

It may also be useful to name areas of particular strength and interest within the profession. Examples include:

Clerk
Accounts Payable, Accounts Receivable, Payroll

Materials Management
Warehousing, Trucking, Air Freight, Scheduling

Business Manager
Bookkeeping, Office Administration, Supervision

Building Engineering
Construction, Maintenance, Fire Protection

Marketing or Sales Administration
Sales Tracking, Market Research, Database Administration, Report Preparation

Finally, your Professional Objective may also include an indication of how advanced you are in the profession. Using words such as Executive, Senior, or Assistant, this also suggests how much you expect to be paid. Examples include:

Executive Director
Financial Development, Program Management, Community Relations

Senior Banker
Commercial Banking, Branch Banking, Compliance, Asset Management

Human Resources Executive
Strategic Planning, Executive Compensation, Organizational Effectiveness

Human Resources Assistant
Benefits, Recruiting, Training

Once you've written a Professional Objective, you need to build a case for it, much as a lawyer does. Before you start a search, building a case serves as a reality check—you make sure you have evidence that you can do that kind of work. Later that same evidence is the basis for your Core Message, including your resume.

Building a Case for Your Professional Objective

Experience—direct or transferable.

Evidence of relevant skills or knowledge: How much? How strong?

Education and credentials.

The easiest way to build a case for your Professional Objective is to show that you have already done that same kind of work. A teacher who has already taught can more easily build a case, as can a financial manager who has already been a financial manager. But it's also possible to build a case for a kind of work you have never done.

EXPERIENCE

Direct experience should be backed up by information showing how *well* you managed the finances or taught classes. Candidates without direct experience often use related experience, showing that they have the ability. So an accounting supervisor might be ready to move up to a financial management job. Or college teaching could be used to build a case for corporate training.

Transferable experience is past work using similar skills. For example, a teacher's aide who has interacted with children and their parents probably has skills that could be transferred to an aide's job in children's health care or other jobs that require interacting with children and their parents.

TRANSFERABLE SKILLS

Transferable skills require some explanation or "translation." For example, if you want to move from teaching to health care, you can explain the transferable skills you developed in teaching in the language of health care. That way, the Decision Maker will understand them and see their value in a hospital. Sometimes transferable skills gained through life experience are also useful. Caring for your aged parent, for example, might help you get some health care jobs.

In addition to skills, knowledge can also be transferable to new fields of work. In either case, you need to understand the new field well enough to explain how the skills or knowledge apply to that field.

EDUCATION AND CREDENTIALS

Education, special training, and credentials can also be useful if you haven't done the exact same work before. The education could be training on a particular software, a college degree in chemistry, or a Harvard MBA. Credentials could include anything from a nursing license to a CPA designation.

If you have any relevant education or credentials, you will certainly want to use them to build your case. Sometimes people who want to make a large change need to get additional education or credentials to strengthen their case.

THE SHORT COURSE ON CAREER COUNSELING

To sum it up, you need to define a Professional Objective consistent with who you are, and then see how much evidence you can provide that you would be good at that kind of work. That's my short course on how to be your own career counselor.

None of it is a mystery, really. It's a matter of asking yourself some questions and starting with what interests and attracts you, in order to get a tentative description of your next work. Once you have listened to your internal messages, it's time to check them with the external real world to see if they're practical.

If you have an idea you really like but it looks impractical, don't give up on it too quickly—talk to people, pursue it and see if you can shape it into something workable. If you're still not clear about what kind of work to look for, it's worth some more effort. Here are some suggestions on how to do that.

Additional Resources for Choosing Your Next Job

Career planning books.

Discussions with knowledgeable people.

Inventories, instruments, and informal questionnaires.

Career counseling.

If you started with a lot of questions about what kind of work you want to look for, this chapter may not be enough to answer them all. In that case, you might want to try one of these additional routes: career books, talking to people, inventories and instruments, and professional career counseling. Here are suggestions on how to use these routes.

A great first step is reading a book or two on career development and making career choices. This kind of book may include written exercises designed to help you clarify your interests, skills, values, personality assets, and how these relate to career choice. There are dozens of books available on these topics.

Second, talking to people who actually do the kind of work you are considering is invaluable. I strongly recommend this for recent graduates considering what kind of career to pursue. It is also useful for experienced people considering a major career change. In either case, actually visiting the person in the workplace is the best way to go, if it is possible. This technique is sometimes called "information interviewing," but I don't like the name since it's a bit misleading. This is not a job interview, it's an informal talk.

There are numerous career-related psychological instruments, inventories, and informal questionnaires. These typically involve answering a series of questions, followed by some sort of scoring that adds it all up into some useful suggestions. Questionnaires are the informal version and often appear in career books. Instruments require discussion with a psychologist or trained career counselor.

Career counseling is generally unregulated, meaning that people can do it without any particular education or passing any test. If you decide to spend the money to use a career counselor (they can cost $50 to $250 per hour), you should get a recommendation from someone who knows that particular counselor, just as you would if you were choosing a doctor or lawyer.

Please do not buy a large career services package unless you're quite sure you will get good value—and can afford it. There are organizations that sell these packages for thousands of dollars, payable at the outset. Some of these organizations have been caught using fraudulent sales methods and providing poor services. Others provide a good service.

So if you use a career counselor, play it safe. Go with a person or organization that was recommended by someone you trust. Or pay by the hour, so you can pay only for those services that you need and you can stop whenever you want to.

I think that most people willing to work on it can get things figured out by reading and talking to people. There are specific suggestions on additional resources at www.highlyeffectivejobsearch.com. Talking to people may also help you locate an opportunity while you're figuring it out.

As you use any or all of these means to clarify your Professional Objective, you may also find yourself thinking about *where* you want to work. This is your Target Market, which we'll cover in the next chapter.

ORVILLE'S JOURNAL

JESSIE AND I DISCUSS HER NEXT JOB, WHILE A BAG LEAKS IN MY CAR

I was unloading bags of groceries from the trunk of my car. Jessie walked up and immediately launched into it: "I came up with three Professional Objectives. Number one is just like my last job—I liked it. Number two is similar to my last job. So I combined them into one Professional Objective. Was that the right thing to do?"

"Yes," I replied, setting the heavy bag back down in the trunk, but still holding the lighter one. "You don't want to have a lot of Professional Objectives. It makes your search too complicated."

"The last one is teaching," she continued. "Elementary teaching. I've always wanted to do that, but I haven't thought about it for years. Maybe now is the time. What do you think?"

"You seem excited," I said. "It sounds like you like the idea a lot."

"I do," Jessie continued. "It would be second or third grade. Not too young. Not too old. It's such a great age. I can just see all their bright little faces, smiling up at me. But I don't have a certificate."

I set the other bag down. "I know you have a college degree. Do you have any education courses?"

"Yes," she replied, "a couple. I was thinking of majoring in education, but then I switched."

"Do you know what else you'd need to do to get certified?" I asked.

"No. Do you think I should look into it?'

"Absolutely," I said, "but tell me something else. Did you like your work in business?"

"Yes. Yes, I did." she answered. "If they hadn't shut the place down, I would have stayed there for years."

"Which do you like better, that or teaching?"

"Well, the business job pays more," she said, "but I keep seeing those beautiful little kids ... "

"Running around screaming and throwing things." Ben walked up behind her and finished the sentence.

"Hi, Ben," Jessie said brightly. "I know I'd have to manage discipline in the classroom. But I can handle 20 or 30 kids. I handle you, don't I?"

"Yes, you do, dear. And very well." he replied, adding, "I suppose we could handle the pay cut."

"But I'm not sure it's the right time," Jessie said. "It's a big change."

"Why don't you pursue both of them for a while?" I suggested. "Keep looking for that business job. And check into teaching at the same time. Find out what it'll take to get a certificate, how much it pays, and you know, all that. You don't need to decide now. And you don't need a teaching resumé just yet."

"You're right, Orville, that's just what I'll do. My job search in business is shaping up pretty well right now. I have a Target List."

"A Target List? Already?" I smiled. "You're not supposed to do that until the next chapter."

"Well," said Jessie, "when I thought about teaching, I started thinking about how many elementary schools were close enough to drive to. Then I realized that there are private schools as well as public schools. Then I got to thinking about business jobs and realized there are a lot more businesses around here than I thought. Then—"

"Whoa, honey, slow down," said Ben. "Orville doesn't need to hear it all right now. He's got groceries to put away."

"Oh, Orville," Jessie said, "I'm sorry. I was getting carried away."

"I think it's great," I said. "It sounds like you're seeing a lot of new possibilities. In business, and in teaching too."

"Yes I am," she replied, "and if you're willing to stay another minute, I have one more question."

"No problem, "I said. "What is it?"

"How do I find out more about teaching?"

"Do you know any teachers?" I asked.

"No," she said. "Well, yes, sort of. My cousin Kate has a son in Palmer Elementary right now. I saw Jimmy the other day and that's what got me started thinking about teaching. Kate has to know some teachers over there."

"A guy I work with is on the North Orange school board," added Ben.

"Why not start with Kate and who she knows," I suggested. "I'd save the school board person until you know a little more. And maybe Judy would talk to you."

"Your wife?" Jessie asked.

"Yes," I said, "she used to teach. Some years ago. Before you moved here. She still has friends in teaching."

"I never knew she taught,' said Jessie.

"Well, you never said you were interested before, did you?" I replied.

Jessie and Ben both smiled. Then Ben's face turned serious. "Jessie," he said, "I'm sorry, hon, but there are two serious problems with this conversation."

"Really? What are they?" Jessie took the bait. Then we both noticed Ben's little smile.

"First," he said, "you haven't complained about Orville, not even once. Or his book. Or me. And that's saying something."

She smiled. It was true. Her attitude was different today.

"And second," Ben added, "Orville's ice cream is melting."

I looked down. Sure enough, vanilla was leaking out of one of the bags.

"We've got to talk about Chapter 7, Jessie," I said, heading for the freezer with the messy bag. "I know you've already read it."

"Right," she said.

Your Target Market is defined by:

1	**Geographic location**
2	**Industry or type of organization**
3	**Size (annual revenue or number of employees)**

Using these criteria, you can create a list of employers you might want to work for:	**Your Target List**

CHAPTER SEVEN

Your Target List

I like those do-it-yourself projects around the house. You know, building bookshelves, installing a new garage door, replacing a sagging piece of an old plaster ceiling, fixing a door latch—that kind of thing. I also like tools. Not just a good trim hammer or a solid side-cutting pliers, but also power tools like table saws, routers, and drills.

One thing I learned a long time ago, though, is never to buy those so-called combination tools, the ones you see advertised on cable TV or in catalogs. Once someone gave me a hammer with three screwdrivers in the handle. The handle of the biggest screwdriver was also the handle of the hammer. You unscrewed it. Then you could unscrew the smaller screwdrivers out of the handle of the large one. It was clever, like those nested eggs.

The problem was that none of the tools was any good. They just didn't work right. You couldn't swing the hammer properly because the handle was the wrong size, shape, and weight. It was like trying to drive a nail with a stone: It was possible, but it took a lot of luck and was no fun at all. If you want to get the job done right, you need the tool made for exactly that job.

A central tool in job search, of course, is a resumé. Some people believe that each person can write only one correct and proper resumé.

And that a person's one and only correct and proper resumé is good for pursuing any job on the planet.

I think that's like saying that a screwdriver is just as good as a hammer for driving nails. It's not. You need a hammer for the job of driving nails and a screwdriver for the job of putting in screws.

DIFFERENT RESUMÉS FOR DIFFERENT JOBS

In the same way, you would need one resumé to get a job as a high school superintendent, and another if you wanted to get a job driving school buses. When the school board is considering you for principal, they don't care a whole lot about your driver's license and driving record. And a bus contractor hiring drivers is not likely to care about your master's degree in educational administration. In fact, they'd probably laugh while they threw your resumé away. You wouldn't want to use the same resumé for both jobs.

Now, I am definitely NOT suggesting that everyone should have two or three different resumés. But I am saying that your resumé has to be the right tool for the job. What makes it the right tool? First, everything on the resumé convinces people that you can do the kind of work in your Professional Objective. If you try to make your resumé work for all kinds of jobs, you're trying to create some kind of monster combination tool—like a combination hammer-screwdriver-saw—one that can do anything. It won't work.

DIFFERENT RESUMÉS FOR DIFFERENT AUDIENCES

In addition to talking about one profession—one general kind of work— your resumé also needs to speak to one particular audience. If you want that job as high school principal, your resumé needs to say things in the way the superintendent of schools (and maybe school board members) want to hear them. It needs to speak the language of superintendents and school board members and understand their concerns. If you were a bus driver and wanted that school bus job, your resumé would need to talk to bus contractors. Of course, bus contractors are different from superintendents—they have different needs and concerns.

So writing a good resumé—and conducting a good job search—requires defining your Professional Objective, so you know what to talk about. And defining your Target Market, so you know who you're talking to. And where to find them.

YOUR TARGET MARKET AND TARGET LIST

As you may recall from Chapter 3, your Target Market is the group of organizations you might want to work for, organizations that hire people who do the kind of work you want to do. You might also remember that your Target Market is defined by the geographic location of potential employers, their industry, and their size. You'll use this definition to create a Target List of the employers you most want to work for.

Your Target Market criteria and Target List together give you a clear picture of your target audience, the people you will communicate with throughout your search—in your resumé, in interviews, and in general conversations.

In the Pierson Method, this Target List is a key tool in job search—just as important as your resumé. In fact, it's a good idea to have a tentative Target List before writing your resumé, since the list helps you see exactly who your resumé is designed for. When you write your resumé as a communication to Decision Makers in your Target Market, you will write a much better resumé, because you'll understand who your audience is.

In this chapter we'll talk about how to create and refine your Target List. This will help you prepare for resumé writing and planning Your Core Message (Chapter 8). But the Target List is important in its own right too. We will also look at some of its specific uses—the ways it can increase your odds in search. Remember, a Target List is not a list of employers who have job openings. It's a list of organizations that have people doing the kind of work you want. Organizations that you might like.

At first you may be guessing about whether people in your profession work in a certain targets or industries. That's okay. Make your best educated guesses. Include those targets or industries. Then check it out as you talk to people and collect more information.

Creating Your Target List

Use databases, if possible.

Use directories in print.

Gather information from talking to others

Before we look at the details of creating a Target List, I'd like to say a word about librarians. In my years in career consulting, I have seen many, many career consultants help people find great new jobs. And the most important people backing up those career consultants are librarians. Yes, librarians. The career consulting company I now work for has a staff of librarians at headquarters providing Target Market information for our clients.

I had always thought that librarians were people who organized books in neat rows and stamped cards at the desk. In career consulting, I learned that reference librarians and database librarians are information geniuses. If you can tell them what information you want, they can show you where to find it in those information storehouses called libraries and databases.

All of the large cities in the United States have libraries. Even in these days of tight budgets, many smaller towns still have libraries too. And colleges and universities are famous for having libraries.

The most important thing I have to say about making a Target List is this: Ask your local librarian to help you. Tell the librarian your criteria, the location, industry, and size of organizations you want, and they will show you where to get the list, in a database or in directories in print. Make sure that the librarian knows that you want information on organizations, not on job openings.

DATABASES

If you can find the right database on the Internet or in a library, the easiest way to make a Target List is to enter your criteria (geography, industry, and size) into the database. The database will then create a list for you. You can adjust it by modifying the criteria if you want to. Then you can download it and print it.

While this is a great way of creating an initial Target List in very little time, there's a catch. The best databases—Dun & Bradstreet, Standard & Poor's, and LexisNexis, for example—are expensive, and you may not be able to get access to them.

However, there are other options. There are some good databases free on the Internet—Hoover's, for example—and many smaller more specialized ones. The first step for most people should be the nearest library reference room. Some libraries will give you free access to excellent databases. Larger public libraries in cities are usually your best bet, as are college and university libraries.

DIRECTORIES IN PRINT

Another possibility is using directories in print. While they are slower than databases, there is also an advantage: You may learn quite a lot about your Target Market while browsing in them. One thing you can be sure of is that there is a directory in print that has your Target List in it. Or it may be a combination of two or three directories. If you've clearly defined your criteria, a reference librarian can tell you which directories are best.

For business targets, the best starting point may be a general business directory like Dun & Bradstreet or Standard & Poor's. There are also specialized directories in health care, higher education, law, banks, and anything else you can think of.

You can even find directories of directories—Gale Publishing's *Directories in Print* is an example. For many business people the best directory is a local one, often published by a Chamber of Commerce and available from them or in the local library. There is also a host of local directories for areas other than business, covering government agencies, social services, schools, and many others.

In using both directories and databases, remember that the information will never be 100 percent correct. Most directories are printed once a year, but it might take six months to compile and print it, meaning that the information is six months old even if you use the book on the day the publisher releases it. Databases can be updated more easily, but the people who manage them may actually do the updating only once a quarter or once a year.

But don't worry. Most of the information will be correct. You will find any incorrect information by talking to people and updating it. The best and most up-to-date information always comes from talking to people.

MAKING A TARGET LIST BY ASKING AROUND

You can actually make a Target List without any directories, databases, or librarians.

One of the very best and easiest ways to collect information is the one you use to find a doctor or a babysitter—asking around. Once you've defined geographic area, industry, and size, list out all the examples you can think of. Even two or three is enough to get started. Then show this initial list to your friends and ask them if they can think of others. While you're at it, ask them if they know of directories, Internet resources, or other people who might have additional information.

The ideal way to make your Target List is to start with directories or databases, then refine it by talking to people. These people might also know of new databases or directories for you to use. The combination of the three works very well.

I recommend making an initial Target List of about 40 organizations. If you have trouble finding them, don't worry. Start with five or 10 and keep working on it. Once you have a list, even a short one, start getting acquainted with the organizations on it.

How to Gather Information about Your Targets

Check their Web sites.

Read their publications.

Read articles about them.

Ask around.

Talk to an insider.

As you work on building your Target List, you can also begin getting acquainted with individual target organizations. If you have Internet access, check their Web site. Just about every organization has a Web site these days. Some are only one page. Others might take an hour or two to explore. Web sites of your targeted organizations are always worth looking at because they're written by and about the people you are considering working with.

Most organizations also have brochures, sales materials, or other printed materials. Large businesses whose stock is sold to the public are required to have an annual report and to send it to those who request it. If you are a manager, you may also want to see their required financial statement, the 10K. The organization's Web site may tell you how to get their printed materials.

In addition to what they say about themselves, you also want to know what other, more objective people say about your targets. Sometimes you can find articles in newspapers or journals. Again, a librarian can assist in this. Or you may find information by entering their name into a search engine on the Internet. Once you start showing your Target List to friends and relatives, they may start noticing articles about companies on the list too.

Asking around is a great technique for getting acquainted with targets as well as finding their names in the first place. In fact, you can do both at the same time. One of the less known facts about job search is that talking to people about your Target List is much more useful than talking to them about your resumé.

If you're unemployed, all of your friends should have your resumé, of course, and you may want to discuss it with them. But the most useful conversations are about your targets, what they're doing, what it's like to work there, who works there, who is in charge of what, and similar topics.

What's the very best way of getting information about a target organization? Talk to someone who works there. If you can locate a current or former employee by asking around, you'll have one of the best possible information sources. Insiders, especially when they are friends (or friends of friends), can and will tell you just about anything about their organization—including your Decision Maker's name.

Questions to Ask About Your Targets

What do they do?
How do they do it?
How well are they doing?
What is it like to work there?
What do they expect from employees?
How do they treat employees?
What do they pay for the kind of work you want?
How can you help them?
Whenever you can, ask for:
An introduction to an insider, someone who works there.
Your Decision Maker's name, and an introduction to them.

You need two kinds of information about each of your targets: Information to help you decide if you want to work there, and information to help you get a job there. Often, the same information is useful in both categories.

Once you have the name, address, and phone number of an organization that sometimes hires people like you, you want to learn exactly what they do and how they do it. The better you understand them, what they do and how they do it, the better you'll do in an interview.

As you understand the differences between your target organizations, you can better decide which of them you prefer.

You also want to know what it's like to work there. How do they treat people and what do they pay them? You should always be asking about pay scales for the kinds of work you're interested in. If you do this along the way, you will immediately know whether your first offer is a good one or a weak one because you'll have a clear picture of the "going rate" in your Target Market. This puts you in a much better position to negotiate salary.

Most important, you want to know how you can help them. You want to find ways to put your skills and other strengths together with their needs. You might discover that their relevant needs are as simple as having more employees who arrive on time on Mondays and work a full day on Fridays. Or as complex as needing to turn around a failing $400 million business unit. Every time you discover something you can help with, you've taken a step closer to working for them.

Finally, you want to know the name of the Decision Maker—the person who will be your boss when you work there—and anything else you can find out about that person, from when they arrive at work and how they drink their coffee to their management philosophy and aspirations for the department or company. If you are looking for a management position, the names will be in some of the directories, along with a biography. But everyone discovers the most important information on the grapevine—by asking around. And especially by talking to insiders, current employees.

All of this information is very useful in sorting out and prioritizing your targets.

Prioritizing Your Target List

Choose your top targets because:
You like them.
They have more people employed in the job titles you want.
They are well run and successful.

As you collect information, use it to prioritize your Target List. You may discover things that lead you to eliminate certain targets entirely. You will also learn things about organizations that cause you to jump them up into your top 10. And people may also tell you about organizations you had not considered and want to add to your list. Talk to people about your Target List, staying away from the question of who has openings and who is "not hiring."

Build your list up to 40 organizations, if at all possible. If you live in a small town, don't despair. People find jobs with shorter Target Lists too—especially if the list contains some larger employers along with the small ones.

YOUR TARGET LIST: THE ROLLING 40

You could say that your entire search is about prioritizing and reprioritizing your Target List. In fact, people who use Target Lists sometimes call them the "Rolling 40" because 40 is a good average length and its content is constantly changing.

The best reason to have an organization at the top of your list is simple: Because you like it and know enough to know that you want to work there. In addition, you want to know that they do indeed hire people with your skills and that they're a reasonably well-run organization.

When they have completed their Target List, people sometimes say, "Okay, now I'm going to mail my resumé to all of them." I cringe when I hear this, because, for most people, resumé mailings are a waste of time. The reason for having a Target List is to guide and direct the entire search, whether you use direct mail techniques or not.

Use Your Target List to Find a Job Faster

I cannot overemphasize the importance of creating a Target List and talking to people about it. As you do this, you get educated about possible employers so that later, when you get an offer from one of them, you know where that particular employer fits into the bigger picture. You will know whether or not it's a great place to work. You will know better how to interview and negotiate.

But even more important, you'll find ways to actually get acquainted with your targets and meet Decision Makers and other insiders before there's an opening. This is how you become one of those known candidates we talked about in Chapter 4.

It is even possible that you will "accidentally" find a job while you are creating, prioritizing, and researching a Target List by talking to people about organizations. If so, I wish you the best in your new work, and it's perfectly okay with me if you never read the rest of this book.

Until you do accept a great new job, keep working on your Target List. The more you know about your top targets, the better you can tailor your communications message to them. Delivering a powerful, tailored message in your resumé, in the interview, and in all search communication is a direct result of your work on getting to know your Target Market. It is also the topic of the next chapter.

ORVILLE'S JOURNAL

JESSIE HAS SOME GOOD LUCK WITH HER TARGET LIST

"Your wife did all my Chapter 7 work," Jessie said. "I'm ready to move on to Chapter 8."

"Judy mentioned that you two had talked," I replied. Jessie, Ben, and I were sitting on their deck, enjoying the Sunday afternoon sunshine. It had been several days since we talked.

"Yes," Jessie continued, "she gave me the name of every elementary school within an hour's drive of here, public and private. My entire teaching Target List. From memory. Then she gave me the names of two elementary school teachers she knows. And one retired elementary teacher." Jessie was smiling. So was Ben.

Ben leaned over, letting me in on it. "You better lock your wife up or no one will buy your book."

Now I was smiling too. Judy knows a lot about education—and career management. "I'm in favor of people in job search getting a break sometimes," I said, "and it looks like you got one this time. Did Judy arrange a couple of job offers for you too?"

"Actually," said Jessie, "I'm glad I don't have a teaching offer right now, because I haven't figured out if I want one. Judy said I was qualified for a teacher's aide job right now. I could do that while I took some more courses and got a certificate. But she also told me the pay ranges for aides and first-year teachers. Wow! Was I surprised!"

"It's less than you're used to making?" I asked.

"Yes, and not just the aide jobs, the teaching jobs too," she said. "But I still keep seeing those cute little kids."

"Well, Jess," said Ben, "they get a new crop every year. They'll still have an elementary school next year and the year after. No shortage of cuteness."

"I know," said Jessie, "but I'm not sure. I might rather work in business a little longer. Maybe I can take education courses while I'm working there. I'm just not sure."

"She has a great business Target List," Ben told me with a touch of pride. "I saw it. Twenty-four companies."

"Ben not only saw it, he thought of six targets for me," Jessie added. "Good ones."

"But you know who gave her even more targets than I did?" Ben asked. "Her old boss, the guy who fired her."

"That's not fair, Ben," Jessie said. "Tom got laid off too. Anyway, he gave me four names—all competitors or suppliers of our old company. And he gave me the names of two Decision Makers he knows. He said he'd recommend me to all of them."

"Six names!" I was impressed. "That's outstanding!"

"I told her not to talk to the Decision Makers yet," said Ben. "She should talk to some other people in the organization first, don't you think, Orville?"

"Sometimes that's a very smart way to do it," I said, "but it depends on how much you already know, Jess. Maybe you learned enough from Tom to go ahead."

"I think I should do a little more research first," Jessie said. "I should talk to them even if there's no job opening, right?"

"Definitely," I replied.

"That's in Chapter 3," Ben noted.

"But what if I want a teaching job?"

"Talking to Decision Makers doesn't mean you'll get a new business job right away," I replied. "And there's no law against turning offers down. I think you should talk to Tom's friends as soon as you feel ready."

"You mean when I've read their Web site, checked out the company, and maybe talked to someone who works there?" Jessie asked.

I smiled. "Yes. Exactly right. If you can find someone at your level who works there, that can be a big plus. If not, I think you'd want to talk to them before too long anyway."

"I think so too," said Jessie, "but I still like the little kids. I'm going to talk to Judy's teacher friends. They sounded nice."

"Jessie," I said, "you're sure busy with your search these days."

"Yes," she said. "Sometimes I even enjoy it."

**Your Core Message tells your
targeted Decision Makers that:**

1	You can **do the work** defined by your Professional Objective.
2	You can do that kind of work **well**.
3	You offer **something different** from (or better than) others who do the same work.

CHAPTER EIGHT
Your Core Message

We sometimes hear news stories about people who were caught lying about their abilities by inventing experience, jobs, or degrees. But in all of the thousands of people I've talked to in search over the years, I can remember only one who exaggerated his qualifications. He wore a gold lapel pin that said *#1* and told me immediately that it referred to him.

Other than that one guy, everyone I've talked to politely understated their value. Sometimes very seriously. I nearly always discover that people have much more to offer than they initially tell me. This concerns me because understating qualifications can make the search longer. And result in a lower salary.

I believe there are two reasons why people understate their value. First, in normal conversations, modesty is a virtue. While people are sometimes justifiably proud of their work, most don't brag. Second, most adults have gotten better at doing certain kinds of work without realizing it. When they accumulate skills through experience, they often do not have a name for the skills. And they may not have a way of gauging the strength of those skills.

I am personally opposed to lying—in life or in a search. I also think exaggerating is more likely to harm your search than to help it. However, I'm very much in favor of your telling people exactly how good you are at doing the kind of work defined by your Professional Objective.

This means that it's important for you to label and describe your skills and other strengths. It may at first *feel* like you're bragging when you describe your strengths accurately. But you need to persevere and create a Core Message that honestly tells everyone what you have to offer. Talking about yourself in search is very different from how you normally talk about yourself.

LEAVE OUT THE NEGATIVES

It is your job in search to tell everyone exactly how good you are. And while you're doing that, it's also a good idea not to shoot yourself in the foot by including any negatives about anything. Let me give you an example of this.

I once worked with an unemployed man named Andy. He had been let go, along with 1,999 other people, by a large well-known company that was doing a global downsizing. His last job was a good one, a management job. He was an above-average performer, but he'd been looking for a new job for four months, with no interviews and no Decision Maker contacts at all.

Part of the problem was that he didn't have a Project Plan. But an equally serious problem was what he said when I asked a few questions to check his Core Message:

Me: Tell me a little about your background.
Andy: Well, I got fired by United Amalgamated. My boss just called me in one day and said that was the end. After eight years of working there! Can you imagine? I felt like whacking him.
Me: Okay. I understand that you were caught in the UA layoff. Can you tell me a little about your experience, your work background?
Andy: Sure. I worked for UA for eight years. And for two other companies before that. I worked my way through college as a waiter. I have about 15 years experience. The last six years were in management jobs.

Take a careful look at what Andy said. In 73 words, he gave at least two reasons for Decision Makers not to consider him. His first five sentences were all negative. He didn't get to his best information until the last sentence. The word "management" was the seventy-second word out of 73.

Working his way through college says good things about him, but after 15 years of work experience, it's certainly not his greatest asset. He never mentioned his recent job titles or any successes. It left me worried that people would remember him as a waiter rather than a manager. Unfortunately, he had already said similar words to dozens of people. Now he would need to work hard to undo the damage.

People in job search often repeat themselves—it's part of the job of search. People who begin a search without preparing often end up repeating messages that are not very useful—or, even worse, that are damaging, like Andy's. It's not just those caught in layoffs who do it. It's quite common for people to say things like:

"I've been having a lot of trouble at work lately, so I have to make a move."

"I don't have much experience. Only five years."

"I've been unemployed for seven weeks and I'm desperate for a new job. I'll pretty much take anything I can get."

Negative messages like these can only hurt you. And saying such things to all your friends and acquaintances is almost as damaging as saying them directly to employers.

CREATING YOUR CORE MESSAGE

Your Core Message is your overall plan for what you will say about yourself in your search and how you'll say it. It needs to be honest, carefully planned, and completely positive. It should focus on the needs of Decision Makers in the kind of organizations you've targeted—and on what you have to offer them, covering all of your important selling points.

Although you may later tweak it for a particular Decision Maker, your message about what you have to offer needs to be generally consistent, no matter who you're talking to. Information you give to friends and acquaintances will sooner or later be repeated to insiders and Decision Makers. This is exactly what you want to happen. So help them out by preparing a strong Core Message for them to use.

Have you ever noticed how television advertising repeats the same simple message again and again? There is power in repetition. You need to prepare a focused, honest message about how good you are in doing the work defined by your Professional Objective. Then repeat it again and again. Put that message in your resumé. Use it in interviews. And pass it along to everyone you talk to.

Even though you will use it with everyone, your Core Message is directed first and foremost to Decision Makers in the organizations described in your Project Plan. If you do not know how they think and what they see as important in employees, you should talk to some people who do.

Focus on What Makes You Good at Your Professional Objective

No one is good at doing all of the thousands of jobs that exist in today's complex world. People who say they want "just any job" would actually turn down many of them, and would not be qualified for most of them anyway.

The key to a successful Core Message is focusing on the group of jobs defined by your Professional Objective. Even if you've never had those particular job titles before, your Core Message is intended to provide evidence that you can do that kind of work. You should mention skills, experience, abilities, knowledge, accomplishments, education, or personal characteristics you possess that are relevant to that particular group of jobs.

Convince people that you can do that kind of work well

If you've had job titles identical to those you are seeking, or experience that is obviously relevant, that should be a central piece of your Core Message. But in addition to showing you can do it, you should also show you can do it well.

Often, the most convincing evidence of your effectiveness is a story about a past success in similar work. In the career field, we refer to these stories as "accomplishment stories." These are rarely events that were written up in the newspaper. They may or may not have been recognized by your boss. But they are very important in getting a new job.

These are the everyday stories of how you've done particular parts of your job well, or solved problems that came up, or how you went the extra mile on something. They illustrate your skills. Rather than saying, "I do outstanding work," you tell a story to make that point. When you have prepared them, they can always be told in one to two minutes.

You will probably not be using these stories with your friends and acquaintances (unless they've agreed to repeat them to others for you). But you should definitely use them with insiders at targeted organizations and with Decision Makers, to illustrate your ability to do the job.

WHAT MAKES YOU UNIQUE?

In addition to letting people know that you are a skilled salesperson (or accountant or general manager), it's useful to let them know what makes you unique, and maybe more interesting than others who do the same kind of work.

For example, you might be the salesperson who is acutely aware of profitability as well as sales volume. Or the salesperson who not only get accounts, but keeps them through thick and thin. Or you might be the accountant with broad experience in selecting new software. Or the general manager who is particularly good at turning around weak or failing businesses.

Your Core Message Guides All of Your Communications

Resumé writing
Informal conversations with anyone
Formal job interviews

Once you've developed a Core Message, use it to guide all your communications, especially your resumé, interviews, and the many conversations you have with people in general.

YOUR RESUMÉ IS YOUR CORE MESSAGE IN WRITING

A good resumé effectively advocates you for the jobs defined by your Professional Objective. It puts the most emphasis on the experience, skills, knowledge, and abilities most relevant to that group of jobs. It includes accomplishments that illustrate these and perhaps point to some unique qualities. It speaks the language used by the organizations on your Target List.

Your best resumé is your Core Message written on paper. If you make big changes in your Professional Objective or Target Market, you will probably need to adjust your Core Message and resumé accordingly. You could write a dozen different honest resumés. But you only need the one that best supports your Project Plan.

YOUR CORE MESSAGE GUIDES ALL SEARCH CONVERSATONS

Your Core Message can also be summarized as a two-minute verbal statement crafted to convince Decision Makers in your chosen Target Market that you can do the work defined by your Professional Objective. The statement consists of your most relevant experience, skills, education, training, and credentials. This two-minute statement may also appear in briefer written form as a six-line "background summary" at the top of your resumé.

You should practice using this two-minute statement in conversation in a relaxed way, so it does not sound "canned." The verbal version can also be boiled down to a one-minute or even 30-second version. It can be used with everyone you talk to in search.

In these informal conversations, you will use a very brief version of your message, but the content is still the same. If someone asks "What's new?" or "What's up?" part of your answer should be, "I am looking for a new job. The kind of work I have in mind is (Professional Objective), because that fits well with what I've done in (30-second Core Message). I'm particularly interested in checking out organizations like (mention some sample targets)."

YOUR CORE MESSAGE IS A CENTRAL PART OF JOB INTERVIEWS

It's your job in the interview to tell the Decision Maker how effective you will be in the job they have, whether they ask the right questions or not. Your answers to questions should always be consistent with your overall Core Message, and should include accomplishment stories. The interview is where you can use those extra accomplishment stories that didn't fit on your resumé.

Everything you say in the interview must build your case that you will be effective in the particular job you are interviewing for. You created your Core Message to display your strongest offerings in your chosen field of work. You practiced it throughout your search. All this work pays off in better interviews.

Creating Your Core Message

Step 1: Make an accomplishment list and analyze it for skills.

Step 2: List the three to six skill areas that best support your Professional Objective.

There are five steps in creating your Core Message. We'll start with two that deal with skills and accomplishments.

A great way to get started on a Core Message is to build an accomplishment list. This classically successful approach has been used by hundreds of career counselors and is described in many career books. It works like this: First, think about things you have done at work (you can also include accomplishments outside of work) and list at least 10 experiences where you've done something well, are proud of it, and enjoyed doing it.

Work with someone who knows you to analyze each of these experiences to see what skills you used. Make a list of skills demonstrated by each accomplishment. Then consolidate the lists and organize the skills into three to six categories.

If, for example, your overall skill list included the similar skills of convincing, influencing, selling, and motivating, you might name that cluster "Sales Skills." Or if your skills included planning, organizing, supervising people, and budgeting, you might put those in a cluster called "Management Skills."

In doing this exercise, you are likely to find categories of skills that you use repeatedly and enjoy using. These are your central or "motivated" skills. This exercise can help you determine a Professional Objective (based on those skills) and to simultaneously build a case that your skills support your objective.

If you are already clear on a Professional Objective similar to your past work and simply want evidence of your ability to do it well, you don't need that last exercise. In this case, make a list of accomplishment stories for each job you have ever held. Each of these can be titled, "The time when I ... " These stories may be of some unusual accomplishment, above and beyond your job description. More often, however, they simply illustrate your particular ways of doing the job well. They create a picture of you at your best at work.

These accomplishments may be something you did in a very short time (like handle an angry customer on the telephone and reestablish a friendly relationship) or a project that lasted months or years (like buying and installing a complex new computer system, introducing a new product, or starting a new organization). They always end with a statement of the results you produced that benefited the organization.

In general, you should list five accomplishments for every $10K of salary you expect to earn on your next job, to a maximum of 40 stories. That means 10 accomplishment stories if you plan to earn $20,000 per year, or 40 accomplishments if you're looking for $80,000 or more. That might sound like a lot, but you'll use them in both resumé writing and interviewing.

Each story is evidence of one or more skills. You should inventory the skills suggested by the stories, then select the three to six skill categories that best support your Professional Objective. If you're not clear on how to do this and want some assistance, come to my Web site, www.highlyeffectivejobsearch.com, and I'll suggest some books that might help.

These accomplishments are not usually things that were written up in the newspaper. They are simply illustrations of how well you do your job. They can be about your normal good performance or about times when you did something above and beyond the job description.

Creating Your Core Message

Step 3: Illustrate each skill area with accomplishment stories.

Arrange your accomplishment stories in the three to six skill categories you selected, so when an interviewer asks about a certain skill, you have several stories to tell about it. Six to 12 of these accomplishment stories can be "bullet points" under various jobs on your resumé. On the resumé, they are not told in full, since they occupy only two to four lines each. If you're asked to elaborate on them at an interview, congratulations, that's exactly the kind of question you want to answer.

You should be prepared to use any of your accomplishment stories in response to interview questions and be able to tell each in one to two minutes. Trained interviewers frequently use "behavior based" interviewing techniques, in which they ask questions that start, "Tell me about a time when you ...." Since your stories are all about "a time when I ... " you are well-prepared for even the best of interviewers. With untrained interviewers, look for ways to illustrate any answer with a well-chosen accomplishment story.

You will never use all of your accomplishment stories in one interview, but preparing a number of them allows you to choose the right one for the right occasion. Your library of accomplishment stories also allows you to expand on skills suggested on your resumé but that haven't been fully fleshed out.

Creating Your Core Message

Step 4: Thinking like a Decision Maker, list your strongest qualifications for your Professional Objective.

Your best qualifications are usually in one of these categories: experience, skills, education, credentials, personal characteristics, motivation, and interest. Let's look at each.

EXPERIENCE AND SKILLS

Decision Makers nearly always look for certain skills and abilities. The easiest way for them to do this is to inquire about your past jobs and employers. If your past experience is obviously similar to the work you're seeking, this may be easy for you too, and an opportunity to use some accomplishment stories to show how effective you were in the past.

If you are looking for a job with a job title you have not yet held, you'll need to work a bit harder, describing your skills so the Decision Maker can see that they are transferable to the new job. Again, the right accomplishment stories will help.

EDUCATION AND CREDENTIALS

In some cases, you will also need specific education or credentials, such as a license or certification. While most jobs do not require these, there are some jobs for which you cannot legally be hired without proper credentials.

If you discover that you don't have the right credentials, don't despair—ask around to see if there are any loopholes. Sometimes you can start work without all of the required credentials if you have some of them and are working on obtaining the rest. Sometimes you can get on Decision Makers' short list by letting them know you're in the course and close to getting the certificate.

The majority of jobs, of course, require no specific education, though most employers see a college education as a plus for salaried jobs. Sometimes the right experience can be substituted for education or training. And if you have a degree that your Decision Makers like, make sure they know about it.

PERSONAL CHARACTERISTICS

More often than most people realize, candidates are hired because they are "the right person," rather than because they have the right skills. This can be because they were introduced to the Decision Maker by a trusted acquaintance. Or it can be because of certain personality characteristics. For example, a Decision Maker who needs someone for a supervisory job may favor candidates who have a warm, friendly way of talking to people, as well as the ability to be firm and assertive.

While personality characteristics can be displayed in accomplishment stories, usually the best way is to have the Decision Maker actually meet you—or at least talk to someone who knows you well.

If your personality is a particularly good fit with the kind of work you're seeking, it's important for people to meet you as well as hear your Core Message. You cannot effectively convey personality in a resumé or by describing yourself—people need to experience you or hear from someone who has. Everyone needs to make talking to people a major search activity. Those whose personality is an important job-related asset (such as sales, teaching, or management) have even more to gain.

MOTIVATION

Decision Makers often consider motivation, though in different ways for different jobs. In lower paying jobs, the question can be as simple as, "Will the person be on time for work? Will they meet the minimum requirements?"

In higher paying jobs, the question is, "How hard will the person work to achieve organizational goals?" Someone can be very skilled and still not push very hard to make things happen. A manager's or salesperson's interest in performance-related incentive compensation is generally taken as a sign of motivation. Decision Makers are often looking for other clues as well.

Motivation is not something you can claim just by saying, "I'm highly motivated." You also need to illustrate it with accomplishment stories, and possibly have those validated by references.

INTEREST IS YOUR TRUMP CARD

Finally, a strong, genuine interest in the particular job or organization is always a huge plus. If a Decision Maker has the choice of hiring a highly skilled candidate who seems bored by the job or a candidate with average skills but a burning desire to do the job, they will usually pick the interested person. Wouldn't you?

Interest cannot be displayed on a resumé. It can only be shown by how you behave and the attitude you display in the interview. People who have taken the trouble to find out about the job and organization beforehand can more easily convince someone that they're interested. People making an effort to meet a Decision Maker who has no current opening are showing a very strong interest.

Displaying your interest can be even more important than describing your skills and experience, but again, you cannot do it on a resumé. You can and should do it in conversations with everyone. Interest is the trump card in the hand of every job seeker. And enthusiasm, when it's authentic and not overdone, is even stronger.

So think of interest as part of your Core Message: Focus your search on work you are truly interested in. Gather the information you need to talk about your interest in an informed way. Do this with everyone and you will automatically be more appealing.

Creating Your Core Message

Step 5: Consider what liabilities the Decision Maker might see or imagine.

It doesn't matter what you think your liabilities are (unless what you think is undermining your confidence). What matters are your perceived liabilities—what the Decision Maker thinks your liabilities might be. To accurately assess that, you need to think like a Decision Maker. You may also need to talk to others about it, people familiar with Decision Makers in your field.

Decision Makers often look at the whole skill picture of a candidate and see the least developed of the needed skills as a liability. It's a tendency to see the hole rather than the doughnut. If you're a bit weak in one expected skill area, be sure you are stating that one as clearly and strongly as you can. Don't be defensive. Tell them what you have, not what you don't have. You might want to practice this with a partner, to make sure you're describing the entire doughnut.

Many perceived liabilities have more to do with the Decision Maker's prejudices than with reality. Nonetheless, it's your job to deal with them. There are two ways. The first is to find target organizations that do not see the issue as a liability. For example, some Decision Makers might see youth as a liability for managerial jobs—whether that makes sense in your case or not. If this "liability" applies to you, it might be wise to particularly focus on targets that already have young managers.

The other alternative is to prepare a response to the perceived liability and use that proactively, even if the Decision Maker doesn't mention it. For example, a person whose native language is Spanish and whose English is not as good might say, "As you notice, English is my second language. I am in an English public speaking course right now. My references will tell you that I was very effective relating to English-speaking customers in my last job."

Another example is the Decision Maker who once hired a young woman only to have her quit in less than a year to have a baby. While Decision Makers cannot legally ask about family plans or even marital status, the candidate is free to volunteer whatever she wants to. A young woman who suspects that the Decision Maker has this fear might be smart to volunteer some reassuring information. Or take that organization off of her Target List.

Flip them over, and many perceived liabilities have a corresponding asset. Some employers are prejudiced against older workers, for instance, but older workers often have better judgment and better attendance—and you cannot get 25 years of experience in a 22-year-old candidate.

REFINE YOUR CORE MESSAGE AS YOU GO

Listing skill categories and linking them with accomplishment stories is always a good way to start building a strong Core Message. As you learn more about your Target Market, you will refine how you name your skills and tell your accomplishment stories.

It is also important early on to make a prioritized list of your best selling points, combining accomplishments with other evidence to build a strong case for your candidacy for the jobs suggested by your Professional Objective. Again, as you become more familiar with your Target Market, you will refine this list. The key point, of course, is using the evidence and language that is most appealing to your chosen Decision Makers.

In creating and refining your Core Message, it's useful to discuss it with friends and acquaintances—preferably those who can be objective about you and who know something about your Professional Objective and Target Market. And remember, always think like the Decision Maker.

Once you have planned your Core Message, write it into your resumé, practice it out loud, and use it in all search-related communication for the duration of your search: resumé, e-mails, letters, casual conversations, and interviews.

To sum it up, your Core Message is what you say to your Target Market about your qualifications for your Professional Objective. These three—Professional Objective, Target Market, and Core Message—form your Project Plan. Once your Project Plan is drafted, the next step is doing a Reality Check on it. You probably won't be surprised to hear that the Reality Check is the topic of the next chapter.

ORVILLE'S JOURNAL

WE ALL DISCUSS CHAPTER 8, BUT NOT MUCH, SINCE OTHER THINGS ARE HAPPENING

Jessie and Ben had cancelled our meeting to talk about Chapter 8 so they could go out to dinner. Now we were all sitting in the local coffee shop.

"I got a job offer," Jessie said as soon as we had placed our orders. "Well, sort of."

"You sort of have a job offer?" I asked. "What does that mean?" I wondered if that had been the reason for their sudden dinner date.

"Well, they haven't actually made the offer yet, but they've pretty much promised to make one in a week or two."

"That's great," I said. "Tell me about it." I've heard this story before. Sometimes the offer is actually made and accepted. Sometimes not. A great conversation and accepting a job offer are two different things.

"It's one of Tom's friends," Ben put in, "a manager at Western, one of her old company's competitors."

"Yes," added Jessie, "her name is Francine. She's been a manager at Western for years. Tom and his wife are friends with Francine and her husband. So when Tom told her about me, she wanted to meet me right away. We had lunch. She has an opening coming up very soon. It's like my old job. I actually think Western is a better company."

"That sounds very good," I said. "And you like Francine?"

"Yes, I do. I like her a lot," said Jessie, who was glowing now. "I checked her out with a friend of mine who used to work at Western. Everybody says she's a great boss. Fair. Thoughtful. Pleasant. And she says the job will pay a little more than my old one."

"You would have been proud of her, Orville," Ben said. "She used Chapter 8 to prepare for the interview. She wrote out accomplishment stories from all of her old jobs. We practiced interviewing, and she used the stories to answer questions."

"Francine actually asked one of the questions I practiced with," Jessie added. "I think I did a great job. With the whole interview, not just that one question. I got my Core Message across. I talked about skills. And brought up some of the things I had read on their Web site. But to tell the truth, it wasn't a tough interview. Francine had talked to Tom. She liked me before I met her."

"I thought so too," Ben added. "It was hers to lose, as they say. But still, she hit a grand slam, didn't you, Jess?"

"It sounds great," I agreed. "A great interview. And it sounds like you checked it all out very carefully. Even so, I hope you're still working on your search. You know, just in case."

This was too much for Ben. "Oh, come on, Orville! Don't be such a pessimist. Why don't you just congratulate her? I mean, why rain on her parade?" Jessie had put her coffee mug down. She was staring at me too.

"Look, I don't want to spoil the party," I said. "It all sounds really good. But in search it's not over until it's over. And that's when the offer and acceptance are both a done deal. I've seen too many people lose momentum by assuming it's all done before it really is.

"I hope you'll buy yourself an insurance policy, Jessie. While you wait for this offer, keep looking. You might even turn up another offer. Then you'll have your pick."

"And use the second one to negotiate a higher offer on the first?" Ben asked.

"Well, that's not my first thought in this case," I said, "but it does happen sometimes."

"I know you're worried about this, Orville," Jessie said gently, "but everything's fine. I'm going to have a job in a week. I won't get that much done in a week anyway. In fact, I'd like to invite you and Judy out to dinner with Ben and me. To celebrate. You know, after it's all wrapped up, of course. I really appreciate your help. And hers. Next time I need a job, I might actually go with teaching."

"I'll be delighted to accept that invitation," I replied.

Then three weeks went by and no invitation came. I know that Decision Makers often underestimate the time it takes to get approvals and make the hire. But after four weeks I began to worry.

RECOMMENDATION:

**Before you use your
Project Plan, do
Reality Check on it.**

CHAPTER NINE

How Many Fish Are in That Pond?

Over the years, I have seen more people than I care to remember who have been unemployed for a long time and were having trouble with their job searches.

Usually they're very discouraged, sometimes even depressed. They often feel that they have nothing to offer, that their qualifications are hopelessly weak. They sometimes attempt to deal with this by making desperate moves like offering to take a major salary cut.

The biggest tragedy is when the only problem is their targeting. Like Everett. Once, I worked with a man with that name who had been a financial executive for a railroad in Altoona, Pennsylvania. Unfortunately, the railroad he worked for was reducing its operations in Altoona and let him go.

I don't know if you've ever been to Altoona, but it's a lovely small city on the western edge of the Appalachian mountains in Pennsylvania. Everett didn't want to leave it, and you couldn't blame him. His family were all there, and had been for three generations. He owned a beautiful mortgage-free, custom-built house. The same house in Pittsburgh or Philadelphia would have cost four times what he paid in Altoona.

After the layoff he began his search by looking for a new job as a railroad executive, or perhaps an executive in railroad-related manufacturing industries. He knew there were not a lot of those jobs. But he wanted to stay in Altoona, and he liked the work he'd been doing, so he figured he'd "give it a try."

To see what "giving it a try" means, imagine a large woodland pond. Now imagine that we have X-rayed the entire pond and we know for certain there are only four fish big enough to get their mouth around the average fishhook. A fisherman without our giant X-ray machine might nonetheless "give it a try." But he could easily work that pond all summer and catch nothing. Even with the very best gear and a lifetime of experience fishing, it would take a great deal of luck.

When Everett said he'd give it a try, he was fishing in that kind of pond. If he had made a Project Plan and done a Reality Check, he would have discovered that there were only four jobs like the one he was pursuing—and that they would most likely come open at the rate of less than one a year.

When Everett reconsidered his plans and decided to look for financial management jobs in all manufacturing industries, not just those that were railroad related, and in service industries as well, the odds changed considerably. And when he added CPA firms and other consulting firms to the mix, the numbers shifted even more in his favor.

Had he been willing to move to Philadelphia or Pittsburgh, it would have been like fishing in a well-stocked pond with hundreds of fish—one where anyone with a fishhook and a little bait could catch one. While it was not quite that good in Altoona, Everett got his odds up to a realistic number and found a good new job.

The kind of Project Planning problem that Everett confronted happens to people every day, people working hard to find a new job but making no progress. They feel discouraged that they're not getting any interviews at all. They decide that they are not well qualified. But, in truth, their qualifications are fine. And their search techniques are good. They are simply fishing in a pond with very few fish, tackling an unrealistically small Target Market. They don't understand that no matter how qualified you are, job search is a numbers game.

WHY A FALLBACK PLAN IS A BAD IDEA

Another way people "give it a try" goes like this: They have a Plan A that is a Project Plan they like. It includes their ideal Professional Objective and first choice Target Market. They also have a Plan B Target Market, a bigger one that they also like, but not as well as Plan A. They decide to pursue Plan A only, changing to Plan B as a fallback if Plan A doesn't work.

There are two problems with this approach. The first is: How long should you pursue Plan A before switching to Plan B? If you haven't found a new job in a month, is it time to move to Plan B? Three months? A year? How will you know when it's time to switch?

If Plan A works in a reasonable time, and you find a great new job without ever trying Plan B, everything is great. But if you decide to switch to Plan B, the time you spent on Plan A—whether a week or a year—was wasted. You're starting work on an improved plan later than you needed to.

An even more serious problem lies in the fact that search is all about talking to people. If you start by telling everyone that you're looking only in railroads or only in Altoona, and then later change your plan, what will people think? Some might assume that you discovered you're a weak candidate. Or that you're scattered or disorganized in your approach.

But whatever people think, you've wasted time. If you change your plan, you'll need to go back to everyone you already talked to about Plan A and discuss Plan B. There is some "start-up" time in any search. You would be doing that start-up twice. Why wouldn't you just discuss both plans the first time? Why not work on A and B on parallel tracks, rather than one after the other?

The Pierson Method suggests having a Project Plan with a Target Market you know is large enough, combining A and B from the beginning. Tell everyone about this plan. Then put most of your effort into part A, with less effort into part B. Over time, as you get the A employers covered, you shift more effort to B employers, while continuing to follow up with the A employers. The worst consequence of this approach is that you get an early B offer—that you're free to reject.

EVALUATING YOUR TARGET MARKET WITH A REALITY CHECK

This chapter is about how to evaluate your Target Market by doing a Reality Check on it. Then you'll know how many fish are in the pond. If you don't like what you learn, you can change your plans. By doing this at the outset, you save yourself time and trouble later.

The Reality Check involves answering six questions about your Target Market. Each of these requires making numerical estimates about your chosen Target Market. There is no need to be totally accurate in answering the six questions at the outset—estimates, or even "guesstimates," are sufficient. Many can make these initial estimates based on knowledge they already have.

When you later create a Target List, get the assistance of others who are familiar with the particular Target Market you have chosen, in order to make an accurate assessment of it. As you make your Target List, you will actually count the available targets. You can go to a library and ask a reference librarian to help you select and use the appropriate directories, databases, or other resources. This is your final Reality Check—going beyond estimates to actual numbers.

Let's walk through the six questions. You may want to try it out on your Target Market by making estimates as we go.

Reality Check Question 1

How many organizations meet the geographic, industry, and size criteria in your Project Plan?

If your Project Plan specifies the banking industry in the city of Hunterville, including all branch offices of all banks of all sizes, how many are there? What is the total number of organizations that might employ you?

If you live in Hunterville, you might immediately know that there are three different banks. But without going to the library and looking in the Chamber of Commerce directory, you might not know that each of the three has six branch offices. You could also get that information online, in the yellow pages, by talking to your friends, or by stopping in at one branch of each bank and asking.

If you have completed a Project Plan, how many organizations meet your geographic, industry, and size criteria? Write your best guesstimate on a piece of paper right now. Later you can get more information to check it.

Reality Check Question 2

How many appropriate jobs (not openings) exist right now in each of those targeted organizations?

If you want to be a bank teller in Hunterville, you might estimate (or know) that there are three banks in Hunterville, each with six branches, or 18 places where you could work as a teller. If the average branch had eight tellers, eight is the answer to Question 2. If you want to be a branch manager, the number is one, as in one manager per branch.

If you want to be the president of one of Hunterville's three banks, the number is one per bank, regardless of how many branches they have. And you'd have to find out whether the president was in Hunterville—since that job might be in New York, Chicago, Atlanta, or San Francisco.

We are not asking about job openings right now. We'll get to openings in Question 6. At the moment, we're just taking a step toward determining the size of your personal job market—the number of fish in the pond. We are only looking at the jobs included in your Professional Objective. You may need to estimate the number of appropriate jobs in each organization, based on the total number of employees. You can find the total number of employees in directories in the library. Or you can ask people who are familiar with the industry to help you.

The question here is: On average, how many jobs per organization exist right now? The purpose of this question is to get the answer to the next one, which is the key question. If you can answer Question 3 without answering Question 2, that's just fine. Again, write your number down.

Reality Check Question 3

How many appropriate jobs (not openings) exist in your entire Target Market?

This is the key question: What is the total number of existing jobs in your Target Market? It's the same as asking what is the total number of fish in the pond.

To get the answer, multiply the average number of jobs per organization by the number of organizations. For the bank teller in Hunterville, the total is 18 branches times eight tellers per branch, or 144 jobs. For the branch manager, the number is 18 branches times one manager per branch, or 18. For the president, the number is three, one per bank—if all three banks have a president in Hunterville.

Write your number down.

Reality Check Question 4

How many years does someone typically stay in one of these jobs?

Moving from total jobs to an estimated number of openings requires an estimate of turnover, or how often people leave. How long does someone usually stay in one of these jobs before moving on to something else and creating an opening? Again, this is an estimate. When the banking industry has a lot of mergers and acquisitions, a bank president might stay in the job for only five years, a branch manager for three years, and a teller for two, on average. We'll use those number for the example.

But if the industry is stable and the economy isn't doing well, people might stay in their jobs much longer. It depends on local job market conditions and other factors.

It can be difficult to get accurate information on turnover, but the estimates of people who work in a particular field are pretty good. If you have experience in the jobs and organizations in your Project Plan, make an estimate. In any case, it is something to ask as you talk to people. Bank tellers can tell you how long bank tellers usually stay in the job. It's best to ask several, in several different organizations.

Again, write your number down. If you're not sure right now, make a guess and check it later with people who work in that field.

Reality Check Questions 5 and 6

**How many openings each year are likely in your Target Market?
How many openings each month?**

Finally, divide the total number of jobs (the answer to Question 3) by the number of years someone is likely to stay (the answer to Question 4). This gives you the total number of jobs likely to come open every year in your chosen Target Market. For the bank teller, it is 144 jobs with each person staying two years, so half (144 divided by two) or 72 of the jobs come open each year. This would amount to six per month.

There are 18 branch manager jobs. If branch managers stay three years on average, then one-third of the 18—or six—jobs come open each year. Which is one job opening every two months.

But bank presidents beware! If our estimates are correct, there will less than one job coming open each year. There are fewer jobs at the top of the pyramid. If you are in a high paying job, you sometimes have to work harder to make sure your Target Market is large enough.

The Reality Check: Another Example

Question 1: How many organizations meet the geographic, industry, and size criteria in your Project Plan?

Green County has a total of 32 children's educational organizations of all sizes:

    12 elementary schools
    10 nursery schools
    10 day care centers

Question 2: How many appropriate jobs (not openings) exist right now in each of those targeted organizations?

If you want to be a teaching aide:

    12 elementary schools with 12 aides in each school
    (or 144 aide jobs)

    10 nursery schools with four aides in each
    (or 40 aide jobs)

    10 day care centers with eight aides in each
    (or 80 aide jobs)

If you want to be principal or director, there is one in each school or center.

Question 3: How many appropriate jobs (not openings) exist in your entire Target Market?

144 + 40 +80 = 264 total teaching aide jobs (jobs, not openings)

If you want to be principal or director, there are 32 jobs, one in each school or center.

Question 4: How many years does someone typically stay in one of these jobs?

Aides stay an average of two years; principals and directors stay an average of eight years.

Question 5 and 6: How many openings each year are likely in your Target Market? How many openings each month?

Aides, 264 divided by two, or 132 job openings per year, which is eleven job openings per month.

Principals and directors, 32 divided by eight, or four jobs per year, which is one job opening every three months.

Adding It Up

So what does all this mean? Obviously, the bank president needs to pursue a larger Target Market, just as Everett did. What about the other examples? How many openings each month is enough?

Even if you're a great candidate conducting an excellent search, you will not always be one of the candidates considered. Sometimes you will not hear of the opening—or the organization—until after the job is filled. Even if you talked to the Decision Maker before the opening happens, you may not be considered. The job may go to an inside candidate.

Even though it's illegal, some employers may plan to hire only a man (or only a woman) or only someone over 45 years old (or under 30). The list of what can happen behind the scenes is a long one. The point is that if there are 10 openings a month occurring in your chosen Target Market and you are conducting an excellent search, you might be a candidate in five of them. There are many reasons why it is important to be sure your Target Market is large enough.

Once again, job search is a numbers game—even for those with the best qualifications. Here are some rules of thumb about what numbers are big enough.

The Right Size for Your Target Market

Fewer than 10 openings a month: Expand it now.

Ten to 50 openings a month: Okay.

Over 50 openings a month: Narrow your focus.

If fewer than 10 openings are likely to occur each month in your chosen Target Market, you should expand it. In the branch manager example, with only one opening every second month, the search could go on for years. The teller job is at six openings per month—better, but still dangerously low.

You have several options for expanding your Target Market, described on page 166, and it is important to do it immediately. Like

Everett, you need to be sure your Target Market is big enough—starting on the first day of your search.

If between 10 and 50 openings are likely to occur each month, your Target Market is probably large enough. In our examples, the teaching aide was in this category. These numbers are not scientific facts, but rules of thumb that I created by talking to a lot of professional career consultants.

The actual number is affected by many factors. If your qualifications are strong, you may not need so many openings per month. If your qualifications are below average, you may need more. If your personal job market is flooded with candidates for the kind of work you want, you will need more openings per month. If your job market is one where employers are desperate for candidates, you will need fewer. And so on.

If over 50 openings occur each month, you have defined a Target Market that is very likely to be large enough. With numbers this large, you may want to focus on a narrower geographic area for a shorter commute. Or think more about what kind of organization you would most like and narrow it that way. You cannot be effective pursuing huge numbers of organizations and Decision Makers, so it might make sense to focus on a narrower market.

In all of these cases, you should also consider the number of target organizations. If you are likely to have 25 openings per month but all 25 are with only two employers, there is a higher risk. If 20 of the 25 jobs report to one person and you and that person do not get along, you are left with only five openings per month. More organizations, as well as more potential jobs, lower your risk.

To Expand Your Target Market:

Enlarge the geographic area.

Expand your professional objective.

Include additional industries or types of organizations.

Redefine the size of desired organizations.

If you need to expand your Target Market, do it now!

All of these numbers are simply guidelines. In the end, you must make a judgment on whether your Target Market is large enough. If you have any doubts, you're probably smart to enlarge it. You have four choices for doing that, all based on your Project Plan:

1. **Enlarge the geographic area.** Covering more territory is the most obvious possibility for expanding your Target Market. This does not mean that you have to relocate if you have personal reasons not to. You could consider a longer commute. Or you could choose one of the other options.

   People looking for high-level, high-income jobs sometimes need to conduct nationwide or even global searches in order to have a realistically large Target Market.

2. **Expand your Professional Objective.** Making your objective broader expands opportunities without relocating or having a longer commute. Someone looking for controller positions might expand the objective to financial management. Their Target Market could then include positions such as assistant controller or manager of a specific financial function in larger organizations, as well as that of a CFO in smaller ones. A teaching aide might also consider jobs in health care.

3. **Include additional industries or types of organizations.** A clerk who has worked in banks and targeted only banks might include insurance companies as a second market segment. If the person is a viable candidate for insurance companies, the number of jobs could increase without changing geography or Professional Objective. And there are many other industries with similar jobs.

4. **Redefine the size of desired organizations.** In some cases the size of the organization determines whether an appropriate position exists or not. A Human Resources director, for example, could not work in an organization too small to afford one. But it is sometimes

a matter of personal preference. In that case, you can expand your Target Market by including other sizes. For example, a customer service representative might initially target only the two large well-known companies in town. Expanding to include smaller companies increases the number of opportunities and lowers the risk.

RUNNING A DUAL CAMPAIGN

It is sometimes productive to run a dual campaign, going after two unrelated objectives (such as high school teacher and accountant) in two unrelated Target Markets simultaneously. This dual track search is more complicated than a search with a single objective and may require two resumés. But it's always a safer strategy than devoting time to objective A before pursuing objective B, as we discussed earlier.

I always prefer a single Professional Objective. I don't recommend a dual campaign unless absolutely necessary. In my career, I've probably recommended it to less than 1 percent of my clients.

EVERYONE SHOULD PRIORITIZE

Prioritizing your targets allows you to prioritize your work in the search project. If, for example, you are conducting a national search, it makes sense to list geographic areas in order of preference. Thus, Atlanta might be your first choice, followed by San Francisco, Portland, Oregon, and Philadelphia, in that order. For many people, the numbers are large enough with three to six cities, and there is no need for a true national search. This lets you omit those cities where you do not want to live and focus on those that appeal to you.

If you can work in more than one industry, which ones would you prefer? Listing them out in order of preference allows you to pay more attention to your first choice, say health care, and less attention to your second and third, financial services and retail. The same is true of size and Professional Objective. Getting focused on exactly where you want to work is just as important as getting clear on what kind of work you want to do.

THE JOB MARKET VERSUS MY TARGET MARKET

I often hear people in job search talking about how bad or how good the "job market" is. You may be hearing on the TV news that unemployment is 8 percent and people are having trouble finding jobs. But the truth is, it doesn't matter to you how good or bad the national (or state or city) job market is.

All that matters to you is how good your personal Target Market is. After all, the job market for financial managers in medium-sized firms in Hunterville could be very good, even when the overall national unemployment rate is high. Your personal Target Market could also be worse than the national market, requiring you to make a Project Plan with higher numbers.

As you begin talking to people about your search and your Target List, you'll get information that will help you judge how good your personal market is. If your market is soft, don't despair. Just know that you may need to increase your numbers a bit.

EXPAND IT NOW

Many people make the mistake of conducting a search in a small Target Market with the plan of expanding the market only if it proves necessary. This is a serious mistake. If there is any doubt about whether your Target Market is large enough, please expand it now.

Beyond the six-question Reality Check, there is another kind of Reality Check that is also important, especially for those with Professional Objectives or Target Markets with which they have no prior experience. This involves two key questions: Are you qualified? Is your Target Market the best one for your Professional Objective? Let's take a look at each.

Another Reality Check
Are you qualified for your Professional Objective?

The real question here is whether you will be seen as qualified by Decision Makers in your chosen Target Market. As we have seen, Decision Makers may make choices based more on who the person is than on their qualifications. However, Decision Makers also need to justify their hiring decisions to others, and qualifications are the best way to do that.

A good second Reality Check is to show your resumé and Project Plan to several people with the right expertise and get their opinions. The best person is a current or former Decision Maker in the field of your interest. Other possibilities are human resources professionals, recruiters, or people with experience in the kind of work and/or industry specified in your Project Plan. An experienced professional career consultant could also help.

If you have conversations with three or more knowledgeable people and they all say you are a reasonably well-qualified candidate, your Project Plan passes this test. Please note that you will need to be referred to these knowledgeable people—they will need to be friends or friends of friends. If you try to go to strangers with no introduction, they're not likely to give an opinion on this topic—if they will see you at all.

These same knowledgeable people can advise you on whether your Target Market is suitable for your Professional Objective and qualifications. Sometime early in your search, make a point of getting some opinions and advice on your Project Plan. After you discuss it with a few knowledgeable people, improve the plan if necessary. Then stop asking, because asking too many people this question can be seen as a lack of confidence on your part.

Once you've completed a Project Plan with a Target List and completed a Reality Check on your Project Plan, you're ready to begin your search. The next chapter covers the techniques you can use.

ORVILLE'S JOURNAL

JESSIE GIVES ME THE BAD NEWS—AND THE GOOD

One rainy Wednesday, I was in my office writing a book—this book—when the doorbell rang. It was Jessie. She was by herself, without an umbrella, and looking a bit bedraggled.

"Jessie," I exclaimed. 'You're all wet. Please come in."

"You got that right," she replied. "I'm all wet, all messed up, and I was just plain flat out wrong to ignore your advice four weeks ago."

"Oh, Jess, I'm sorry," I said. "Please, sit down. I'll get you a hot drink. So ... the Francine thing didn't work out?"

"I didn't get the job," she said, looking totally dejected. "They gave it to an inside candidate. Francine stopped returning my phone calls. Then I get this polite rejection letter. A letter! After all those nice talks! I just couldn't believe it.

"Tom—you remember Tom, my old boss?—he told me yesterday that they announced a hiring freeze. Right after Francine interviewed me. She wasn't allowed to hire an outside candidate. She tried to get me, but she had to take someone from inside. Tom said she liked me better but she just didn't know when the freeze would end."

"Did you respond to her letter?" I asked.

"Respond? Respond to what? It's all over. It's done. I'm done."

"That's true for now, but nobody knows what happens next. The inside candidate might not work out. The freeze could be

, Why not send her a nice note?" I suggested. "Tell her you
rstand. You know, let her off the hook. Tell her you'd really
: to work for her the next time an opportunity comes up."

"Orville, you're really a piece of work. You just don't give up,
do you?"

"Of course not," I replied, "and you shouldn't either. I want
to see you in a great new job. I don't know if you'll ever work
for Francine, but why not leave that door open? She likes you.
She might even help you in your search if you asked."

"Okay," she said. "I'll do it. And I apologize for not listening
to you four weeks ago. I should have kept working on the rest
of my Target List."

"Jessie, you don't have anything to apologize for," I said.
"Most people do the same thing. They get their first hot
prospect and that's it. They figure they'll get hired. They stop
looking. They forget that the average search includes five 'hot'
conversations like the one you had. But four of them don't turn
into offers."

"I didn't forget," Jessie said. "I thought I had beaten the
odds."

"Well, I think you actually might beat the odds," I said. "You
have great qualifications. Your Project Plan is good. Best of all,
you're getting better and better at running a search."

"Thanks, Orville. I hope you're right," Jessie said. Then her
face brightened and she added, "I forgot to tell you the good
news. I got a job offer at Northwick Elementary."

"Really?"

"Yes, as a teacher's aide. But I turned it down. I really need to
earn more money right now. But the whole thing helped me see
that I want another four or five years in business. Ben and I
really need to put some money away. Then I want to move to
teaching. I'm going to start working on a teaching certificate as
soon as I start a new job."

"How did you get the offer?" I asked.

"I had lunch with Abby, a teacher friend of Judy's. She told
me there's an opening coming up at Northwick. The aide is

pregnant and planning to resign. Abby talked to the principal about me. Then I talked to the principal, and she pretty much offered me the job on the spot."

"That's great," I said. "You'll probably get a job offer in business the same way."

"Because someone's pregnant?"

"No, because you'll have a referral to the Decision Maker before the opening's announced. You've done it twice now. Keep doing it."

Jessie smiled. "I'm getting better at it, aren't I? And, you know what?" she added. "Yesterday I got back to work. I went to the library and my Target List is up to 44. I did the Reality Check and it comes out 10 openings a month. I think that's too low. But I counted another 38 possibles—smaller companies that I found in the Chamber of Commerce directory."

"Wow! You're really on the move, aren't you?"

"Yes," she said, "and I have a list of about 30 people I'm going to talk to. Show them my Target List and all that. I'm starting with the names Tom gave me." She was heading for the door.

"Well, good," I said, "because you said you're taking Judy, Ben, and me out to dinner to celebrate your new job. I haven't eaten since the day you said that four weeks ago. I'm getting kind of hungry. I have my eye on Freddie's."

"That cheap Italian restaurant? No way. I'm taking you to the best place in town. And soon. But meanwhile, we have to discuss Chapter 10. How about tomorrow evening at my place so Ben can join us? And I'll even give you some snacks, you know, to tide you over."

"Perfect."

Jessie had her hand on the doorknob. Then she turned around.

"Thanks, Orville. I can't tell you how much I appreciate your help."

The Seven Search Techniques

Listed from least important to most important

(SEVERAL OF THESE USE THE INTERNET.)

1. Walking in

2. Cold calling

3. Using direct mail

4. Completing applications

5. Responding to job ads

6. Using staffing firms

7. Networking, or just plain talking to people

CHAPTER TEN

The Seven Search Techniques

The good news about going job hunting is that it is not complicated. You don't need to learn to fly a hang glider, drink water while standing on your head, create an oil painting, or do anything that is particularly difficult to learn. There are only seven techniques used in the actual search. And most people use only three or four of them.

Unfortunately, many job seekers—and even many authors of job search books—get lost in a maze of real and supposed job hunting techniques, especially the innumerable possibilities on the Internet. Sometimes they get so completely lost in the trees that they don't see the forest, much less the path through the forest. They focus only on job openings. They don't understand how to use job search techniques as part of a well-planned search project.

As a lifelong career consultant, my pet peeve is job hunting books written by people who know little or nothing about it. For example, why would anyone write an entire book on how to go job hunting on the Internet? The Internet has been around for years, and so far I haven't seen a single credible study showing that a high percentage of people get jobs that way. And much Internet hiring is just a faster way to do what ads in the paper have always done.

It's good to understand the place of the Internet in search. But some of those books create the impression that the Internet is the key to success in job hunting.

And then there are the networking books. So many misinformed authors have written misleading job search networking books that they have given honest networking a bad name. Some authors confuse networking with a technique called "information interviewing," which is appropriate only for people just starting their careers or working on major career change. Some tell you to be downright dishonest in networking and say you're not looking for a job. And some make networking very complicated, when it's actually something we all do all the time.

Okay, now I'll stop complaining about poor job hunting books. With 2,500 of them out there, I guess they can't all be good. But many of them are quite useful and include more extensive information on the topics in this chapter.

What we're doing in this chapter is looking at the job search techniques or activities people use once they have finished preparing and have actually started their search. We will include both the Internet and networking. But let's start with a question.

WHAT SHOULD YOU DO AFTER YOU FINISH YOUR RESUMÉ?

After you have written that great resumé, should you post it on the Internet? E-mail it to every employer on your Target List? Give it to a recruiter? Check the want ads for places to mail it? Hand carry it to the front office of that special employer you read about?

My answer is simple. You should try the seven search techniques— or at least three or four of them—and see which ones are most effective for you.

No matter which other techniques work the best, just plain talking to people will always help. In the nearly 30 years I have worked with unemployed people, much has changed. Many employers went global. The Internet arrived on the scene. Employment went boom and bust more than once. But people talking to people in job search has been a consistently successful technique—when you find your own best way of doing it. And get over any idea that it's about asking for favors.

By talking to people, you locate the best staffing companies and ad sources. By talking to people you get the information you need to decide which employers you prefer and where your chances are the best. If you have a Target List in hand, talking to people can definitely get you the chance to talk to Decision Makers.

Whether you call this networking or not does not really matter. But I am entirely sure that talking to people is the easiest and best way to move your search along. If you're smart about how you do it, your search will go faster. But even if you were not smart about how you do it, talking to (and listening to) people—especially insiders at your targets—would sooner or later get you employed.

Once you have a Project Plan and have done a Reality Check on it, you need to know what the search techniques are and where they fit into making your plan work. This chapter will give you an overview of all seven and the pros and cons of using each.

In approximate order of importance—from least important to most important, the seven, as listed in the opening of this chapter, are: walking in, using direct mail, cold calling, completing applications, using staffing firms including executive recruiters, responding to job ads, and networking. We'll look at them in order of importance, least to most. You may immediately decide not to use the first three or four—but I want you to know what they are and consider all of them.

You already know that talking to the Decision Maker is the most important thing you can do in search. All of these seven techniques are ways of doing that. Some techniques are more likely to get you in touch with the Decision Maker before there is an opening, so you can be the Known Candidate we discussed in Chapter 4. Other techniques go after the announced "Applicant Pool" job openings. Some techniques are more direct than others; some are more likely to succeed than others.

DOES IT GET YOU A CONVERSATION WITH A DECISION MAKER?

The way to tell if a search method is effective for you is to see if it results in your talking to Decision Makers, or at least insiders at your targeted employers.

Of the seven, networking is the best way to get you the opportunity to talk to Decision Makers before they have an opening. Networking is also a great way to get the information you need to make your decisions on jobs and targets. And the information you need to be effective in talking to Decision Makers when you get the chance.

Job ads, staffing firms, and applications deal only with jobs that are already open—but they can sometimes get you quickly and directly into an interview with a Decision Maker who is trying to fill that opening.

ADS, STAFFING FIRMS, AND NETWORKING ACCOUNT FOR MOST HIRING

Applying for advertised jobs and using staffing firms (including recruiters)—which are about filling openings—are the methods that bring success for nearly one-fourth of job seekers. Networking—which is the best way to get in before an opening—brings success for about three-fourths. The other five methods together account for success for only a small minority of job seekers—but if you are in that group, they are clearly important to you.

WHAT ABOUT THE INTERNET?

"Where is Internet job search?" you might ask. "Even though it accounts for a low percentage of hiring, shouldn't it be included on the techniques list?"

Using the Internet is not a search technique in itself. If by using the Internet you mean going to job boards like Monster and Hot Jobs, that activity is simply another way to respond to advertised jobs. So the technique of responding to ads covers both Internet listings and ads in print. You could say that applying for advertised jobs has been automated by the Internet.

If Internet job search means putting your resumé in someone's resumé database and hoping that the right employer will find it, then we are talking about using intermediaries—people who collect fees from employers for providing candidates. The Internet resumé database works much like the staffing firm's database: Both are intermediaries between you and potential employers.

The real Internet revolution in job hunting is in job market information. For those smart enough to use it that way, the Internet is an outstanding vehicle to find out who the employers are, what they do, and how they do it. This information can make you the smartest candidate who shows up at the interview. And it can help you find the best employers for you.

But I'm getting ahead of myself. Let's look at each of the seven techniques. We'll move quickly though the first few and spend more time on the more important ones.

1. Walking In

Works for some kinds of jobs, but usually not white collar jobs. Very time-consuming.

Sometimes nonunion construction workers get work by driving to a job site in a pickup truck with their tools in the back and presenting themselves to the supervisor. In similar fashion, dishwashers walking into big city restaurants asking for work might have a job before they've walked six blocks.

In both cases the employers' procedure is usually to try them out, letting them go at the end of the day (or sooner) if they don't work out. If you look good, dress right for the job, and sometimes see signs in the window for the kind of work you want, walking in might be worth trying.

Managers—and most white collar workers—who tried this method would soon have people laughing at them. For the vast majority of job seekers this is not a useful method. Among other things, it just plain takes too long. You can telephone 20 places in the time it takes to visit one.

2. Cold Calling

It works for some job hunters.
Most people don't like doing it.

If you are not deterred by having 10 or 20 or 50 people in a row refuse to talk to you (politely or not), cold calling might be part of your plan. It usually works best for jobs that pay by the hour and with employers who have a large number of employees in the job title that you want. It is actually a good technique for many hands-on jobs that pay by the hour, such as bricklayers, installers, fast food workers, and similar jobs. And it can work for salaried jobs.

Another name for this method is "telemarketing." You could also say that it is simply a more efficient way of walking in. It works best when you have a 30- or 60-second script that describes what you have to offer. It requires dozens (or even hundreds) of phone calls, so you need a longer-than-normal Target List. Calling the same employers repeatedly and politely to express interest in working for them is typically part of cold calling.

If you're good at striking up conversations with total strangers on the phone, you can use this method for entry and mid-level jobs. In this case, you could see it as a "cold"—and more difficult—version of networking. It helps to have (or get) the name and title of the person you're calling. Then you present your qualifications on the phone and follow up with a resumé. You may also look at it as a chance to get acquainted, collect information, and get the names of other people to call.

While this method is not a good choice for most people in managerial and other salaried jobs, there are a few who are able to complete dozens—or even hundreds—of these cold calls a week, getting through to enough insiders that they actually get appointments with Decision Makers.

3. Using Direct Mail

Requires a large number of letters or e-mails and an extra long Target List.

Like cold calling, the "hit rate" for direct mail is also a very low percentage. In job search, the average person usually needs to send out at least a thousand e-mails or letters to strangers, usually with a resumé, to get a single invitation to interview. I have actually seen people with good work backgrounds send out 5,000 and 10,000 and get no interviews at all.

Of course, some lucky people—usually with very strong experience or credentials and hot job markets, as well as luck—do get interviews, even with smaller mailings. For anyone, sending letters or e-mails to strangers is certainly better than doing nothing.

But you need to remember that this kind of written communication to total strangers is what you call spam or junk mail when you're on the receiving end of it. Both of them do work, but the response rate is a very low percentage—usually less than 1 percent. If you have an introduction or any kind of connection with the person, you are not doing direct mail. Now it's in the networking category, and the odds are much, much better.

Any direct mail works better when the correspondence is directed to a person by name. (Have you noticed how your junk mail and spam e-mail sometimes has your name on it?) Any direct mail depends on the quality of the written piece, letter, or resumé, being sent. And on the quality of the list you send these to.

Sometimes managers or executives send out mailings of 5,000 or 10,000 letters to a national or global list. These are usually addressed to a top officer whose name appears in a database. If the letters look like well-written personal letters (and not like mass mailings or junk mail) and the resumé is good, this could result in a half-dozen interviews and a job offer or two. But if it does not, you have wasted the thousands of dollars it costs to do that kind of mailing.

4. Completing Applications

Is most important in government hiring.
Can be part of any of the other techniques.
Is sometimes used to get rid of unwanted applicants.

Collecting applications is a simple way for employers to maintain a candidate pool in case an opening comes up. You may be asked to complete an application as part of any of the other six search techniques, sometimes along with a resumé, sometimes instead of one.

The same application process can be a polite way of screening—and possibly getting rid of—job seekers, especially unwanted walk-ins: "Please fill out this application. Thank you. If we have a need we'll call you. Please don't call us."

For some hourly jobs—in retail stores, for example—written applications can be an important part of the process and can sometimes be submitted online. But personal contact with the Decision Maker is still important. If you look good, speak well, or have an introduction, the Decision Maker may very well find your written application and put it in the "interview as soon as possible" stack.

GOVERNMENT APPLICATIONS

Governmental organizations of all kinds are the biggest users of formal application processes at all levels of hiring. Designed to be objective and fair to all applicants by treating them exactly the same, such a process may include tests, work samples, special resumés, write-ups of your skills, and other devices as well as an application. Educational institutions sometimes use a similar formal application process that depends on resumés or that longer, more formal resumé, the curriculum vitae (CV).

The application process for government jobs, especially federal government jobs, can be complex, requiring some real work on your part. It also takes time for the government employer to evaluate these lengthy applications, so you are smart to work on other nongovernmental possibilities at the same time. If government employment interests you, submit as many applications to as many different agencies as possible. There is a numbers game here too.

While government jobs are advertised, the ads are usually found in different places from other jobs. These ads or "notices" are sometimes complex and are sometimes for groups of jobs, not just one.

If you're planning to apply for government or academic jobs and have never done that before, reading a book or two on the topic is a good idea. If you can find an insider to guide you through the process, your odds of success go up considerably. And if you can informally get to know the Decision Maker or someone else involved in the hiring process before you begin, that's even better. In some cases, a Decision Maker can circumvent some steps—or the entire process—in order to hire a candidate they like.

Completing applications for government jobs is the fourth most productive method of search, after general ads, staffing firms, and networking. Completing applications for nongovernmental jobs is usually a variation of walking in or using direct mail—both less productive techniques.

5. Responding to Job Ads
About 10 percent of job seekers find employment this way.
Look to see if your kind of work is advertised.

Ads for open jobs appear in newspapers, professional and trade journals, and on employer Web sites. Internet job posting boards are another place employers can pay to publish employment ads. Let's look at both.

JOB ADS ON THE INTERNET

Employers pay to post ads on job boards, but that's not the only way jobs get there. Many jobs advertised in newspapers and other print media also end up on one or more Internet job boards. Since they want large numbers of listings to attract large numbers of users, the big Internet job boards often use computers to search the Web for openings listed elsewhere to post on their job boards. For the same reason, some may be tempted to leave jobs posted long after they are filled.

The good news about responding to Internet job ads is that you can quickly search huge numbers of them. The bad news is that there is a great deal of competition for them. It is also important to remember that no one Internet job board lists all advertised jobs. And that huge numbers of very good jobs change hands every day without being advertised anywhere.

The larger Internet boards are not always the best place to look. There are hundreds of smaller specialty job boards. If you can find one that covers your Professional Objective or Target Market, that smaller board may be more useful to you than the monstrous boards. Web sites of professional organizations often have job listings and should be included in your search as well. While the job boards account for a small percentage of total hiring, they are more effective for computer-related jobs than other categories.

Don't forget to check ads on the Web sites of organizations on your Target List. You should go to them anyway, to learn more about the employer. While you're there, check their postings.

One last word on the Internet. Since the Internet has become popular, every career consultant I have talked to about it has said it is the job hunter's favorite way to waste time.

Many Internet job sites work very hard to get your attention and get you to stick around and browse awhile. This is good for them because they make more money on their advertising. But it may not be a good use of your time. So use the Internet for information, and maybe for ads—but keep your eye on the clock while you do.

JOB ADS IN PRINT

While Internet job boards pick up listings from many newspapers and other print sources, there are also many job ads in print that do not appear on the Internet. You should certainly check your local newspaper for ads. If you live in an area covered by a big city paper and a smaller local one, check both. If you are bilingual, check any non-English papers that you can read. And don't forget professional journals.

HOW TO RESPOND TO ADS

You should check the Internet and print media for advertised job openings consistent with your Professional Objective and qualifications. If you find some, apply for them. Then regularly check your best sources for more.

As a rule of thumb, if you are applying for appropriate jobs, you should expect one invitation to interview for every 50 resumés you send out to specific individual job listings. If you have submitted over 50 with no inquiries or interviews, you should recheck your qualifications or redo your resumé. If your ratio is better than one in 50, you're doing well.

The usual ad response is a resumé with a cover letter or transmittal e-mail, although most employers will read only the resumé as part of the screening. Pasting the resumé into the body of the e-mail as well as attaching it is a good idea, since some employers prefer one and some the other. Be sure your resumé includes the key words the employer is likely to use in searching the resumé database. If the ads asks for salary desired or salary history, you're probably better off omitting those—unless you're sure that your numbers are in the general range they have in mind to pay.

Do not be concerned if you cannot find ads or Internet listings for the kind of work you want. This doesn't necessarily mean there is a shortage of the kind of job you're looking for. It's more likely to mean that your kind of job is filled through other means.

A final word on ads anywhere: If you see some you are qualified for, apply for them. Don't spend a lot of time writing individual responses, unless you see that "perfect ad."

6. Using Staffing Firms (Including Executive Recruiters)

About 10 percent of job hunters find jobs this way.
Try it.

Employment agencies, "temp" firms, executive recruiters, and other staffing firms are in the business of filling job openings for a fee, usually 15 to 33 percent of the annual salary. This fee is paid by the employer, not you. If anyone asks you to pay a fee, they are *not* a staffing firm, and could even be an illegal operation that preys on the unemployed. If you're talking to someone on the phone and have any doubts, ask them if they charge you a fee. And remember that if they try to duck the question, that means yes.

Executive recruiters concentrate on highly paid jobs, often handling *only* jobs paying more than $75,000 (or even $100,000) per year. The Decision Maker typically pays the recruiter about a third of the annual salary to produce three to six well-qualified candidates. The recruiter collects the fee whether any of these candidates are hired or not. Because the fee is a retainer, these firms are called "retained search."

With fees that high, executive recruiters do not need to handle a lot of assignments each year to make a good living. Many are sole practitioners, working from their homes, in an industry or field where they have a large number of contacts. They have often been employed in a job like those they now recruit for. They nearly always specialize in a particular field or industry. There are also a few very large global recruiting firms with many individual recruiters handling just about all executive jobs.

If you're seeking a high-paying job, you should check directories for recruiters specializing in your kind of work. You should send your resumé to at least 50, since each is likely to have only a few assignments. You want to be in the databases of all of the large firms. If you can get an introduction to one of them, that's even better. Do not expect them to talk to you unless they are working on an assignment that you fit into.

CONTINGENCY AND "TEMP" FIRMS

Other staffing firms, also called "employment agencies," sometimes try to look like the prestigious executive recruiters. But they typically collect a lower fee from the employer—and get paid only if the employer hires a candidate presented by them, which is why they are called "contingency." Agents (sometimes called job or career counselors) are usually paid on commission.

These firms do not have exclusive listings; several staffing firms may be trying to fill the same job. Because they cannot be paid if the employer already has your resumé, you might be smart to get your resumés to your best targets before going to staffing companies. This could allow a targeted employer to hire you without paying a fee.

If you can find staffing firms handling the kind of job you want, you should list with them. If a firm does not promptly get you an interview with a Decision Maker for a job that interests you, try another one. You may need to be listed with a number of them in order to find one that gets you interviews.

You may want to consider "temp" and "temp-to-perm" firms as well. Temporary employment was originally used only with clerical and factory workers. Now it is a way of filling professional jobs as well. Even executive positions are sometimes filled with temporary (or "interim") employees. Some employers prefer to choose nonexecutive permanent employees only from the group of temps already working for them.

With all staffing firms, remember that you do not pay them, the employer does. They work for the employer, not you. So talk to them as if you were talking to a Decision Maker. And keep your eyes open: If they are paid on commission, they may be tempted to try to get you to accept a job you do not want, so they can earn a commission.

Some kinds of work, especially the more common job titles, are often handled by staffing firms. But some employers never use them and some kinds of jobs rarely go to staffing firms, so don't be concerned if this technique doesn't work for you.

But, since it doesn't cost anything and takes so little time, why not try it? Use a directory (or even the yellow pages) to locate firms handling the right kind of jobs. If you're not sure, call them and ask. Get your resumé to them and see what happens.

WITH ADS (INTERNET OR PRINT), AND STAFFING FIRMS:

It's all about your resumé.

You need average qualifications or better.

Your chances are much better if your most recent job is similar to the one being filled.

You need a well-written resumé, suitable for your chosen Target Market.

You must show that you have done the same job, or a similar one, before.

Key words are king.

Your resumé should include the key words important to your chosen Decision Maker.

Key Words Are the Key to Success with Staffing Firms—and Ads

Staffing firms—and ads—rely heavily on resumés. To succeed with these techniques, you should have average credentials or better, which need to be displayed on your resumé in a way that will appeal to Decision Makers in your targeted organizations.

Resumés are frequently circulated electronically and stored in databases. Employers and staffing firms who want resumés often search these databases by using key words. In writing your resumé, you need to think like the Decision Makers in your chosen Target Market. What key words will they search for? Include those in your resumé.

For example, programmers should always include the names of their programming languages, most people should include the names of software they use, and everyone should mention the names of their key skills—using the words the Decision Maker is most likely to use. If your old job titles were unusual but the work was in fact the same as common job titles, you might include the common title in parentheses after the real one, since a key word search is often done on job titles.

Posting Your Resumé on the Internet

When you post your resumé on the Internet, you are putting it in a database of resumés. The database may be searched by employers or recruiters looking for candidates for existing openings. It may also be searched automatically by the Web site's computers in order to match you with listed openings and suggest that you apply—or apply for you.

Once you post your resumé, it may be passed on to other databases. You may not be able to take it back from all of them, so be sure you're happy with it before posting it.

If you do a lot of Internet posting of your resumé, it's also likely that your resumé will be found by people who want to sell you something. Many of them will send you spam e-mails. Some will telephone you. Some may want you to believe that they are potential employers. Some will offer you multilevel marketing or other commission sales jobs on the spot. Some will be honest and some will not. So look before you leap into offers that seem suspicious.

7. Networking, or Just Plain Talking to People

This is the way the majority of people find jobs.
It's a must for gathering information.

When people need information about important matters of daily life, they usually get it by asking around. For instance, parents who need a babysitter usually ask other parents with whom they've had a good experience. Or when you need a new doctor or a dentist, you might ask around. You probably decide which movies to see—or avoid—based on asking around and talking to people. Or which golf club to buy or golf course to go to. We all do this kind of thing all the time, usually without noticing that we're doing it.

When you have a particular question and want to ask around for an answer, you usually start with people you already know. If possible, you start with someone you think might have the answer. So for a babysitter, you go to someone who has young children. If the person you talk to doesn't have the answer, sometimes they suggest someone who might. That might be, "I heard the Smiths just got a great new sitter. Why not call them?" Or if you were planning to buy golf clubs, "Jack just got a new set and his game improved. You should ask him what kind he got."

All of this is networking. Real networking, not the stuff you read about in some job search books. What makes it real is a shared interest between the two people talking to each other. And maybe some kind of connection. The interest could be that they're both parents. Or golfers. Or avid moviegoers. The connection could also be that they're relatives or old friends. Or simply that they both know the same person: "Oh, you know Fran too? Small world, isn't it? How did you meet her?"

COMMON INTERESTS AND INFORMATION

Real networking starts with a common interest. It's what happens at parties. You meet someone, and in the first few minutes you look for common interests. If there are none, the conversation goes nowhere and you go your separate ways. But if you find one, the conversation takes off.

The other thing that happens in networking is that people share information. Information is free, and the more complicated society gets, the more important it is. So adults are always sharing information with each other, on golf clubs, movies, vacation spots, cars, and everything else. The information doesn't have to be on the topic of the shared interest. You might start talking to a golfing friend about clubs but then move on to cars. Or jobs.

What makes it all work is that everyone is comfortable with the conversation, maybe even really enjoying it. When that happens, it has an easy flow. You talk to one person. They suggest another person or two to talk to. If there's enough shared interest there—beyond both of you knowing the first person—the conversations reach out over a broader network.

Networking is all about information. A key question in gathering information is always, "If you don't know, can you think of someone who might know?" And then, "Would you be comfortable introducing me to them?"

THE THREE BIG NETWORKING MISTAKES IN JOB SEARCH

When people use networking in job search, they sometimes forget about the three principles of common interests, information sharing, and everyone being comfortable. Then it isn't networking and it doesn't work.

The most common mistake in job search networking is focusing on job openings and getting hired, rather than on information about targeted organizations, insiders, and Decision Makers. Unless you help them understand it better, many people will assume that the only useful information is who has a job opening right now. Most people simply don't know of any openings and the conversation becomes uncomfortable, even when they want to help.

Along with a focus on openings is the idea of asking for favors. Again, even though you are not asking for favors, people may assume that you are. The big favor in job search is "fixing someone up with a job." In reality, it doesn't happen much. Most people don't know anyone with the power to do it. Most people with the power to do it don't, because it's usually a bad idea.

People who talk to you in job search conversations may worry about whether they're supposed to do you a favor. It's up to you to make them comfortable. If it's not a favor to talk about which movies to go to, it shouldn't be a favor to talk about which employers are the best ones and what they do. And while introducing you to someone might be a favor to you, it won't work well unless it's also a favor to the other person too. In which case all three of you are not only comfortable but happy, right?

Along with job openings and feeling obligated to do favors, the third mistake in job search networking is focusing on the resumé rather than the Target List. People are often comfortable giving resumé advice, and some will give you a lot of it if you ask. The problem here is whether the advice is good (unless they are a Decision Maker or recruiter, probably not) and whether it will move your search along (probably not).

USING NETWORKING—OR JUST PLAIN TALKING TO PEOPLE—IN JOB SEARCH

In spite of all the mistakes made, networking is still the single most effective technique of job search. Even when people use it poorly, it often results in finding a good job.

More precisely, people talking to people is the most effective technique. It does not have to be networking. Over the years, there have been many sociological studies on how people find jobs. Having informal conversations with other people is always the most effective technique. Studies show that this is the case with as many as 75 percent of people looking for new jobs. I use that percentage because it is consistent with my experience.

Finally, studies suggest that people who find jobs that way are happier with the jobs they find and more likely to stay longer. I don't think this is surprising, because people who find jobs by talking to people usually have more information. Along the way, they learn all kinds of things that help them make a better choice of what job they finally accept.

The studies also suggest that you are actually more likely to get the best information from people you do not know well, rather than your best friends. This is often called "the strength of weak connections," illustrating the fact that successful job hunters do not need powerful connections, they just need to talk to ordinary people.

In my opinion, you should start with your best friends, and you may find the information that leads to the job right there. More often, I think, your best friends introduce you to someone else (the "weak connection"), maybe an insider, who provides the critical information or final introduction to a Decision Maker.

The Pierson Method suggests three steps to keep your networking focused and productive: focus on targets, talk to insiders, and meet Decision Makers.

FOCUS ON YOUR TARGETS

First, show your Project Plan and Target List to friends and acquaintances. Make it the main topic of conversation. Ask questions like:

Would you be willing to look at my Target List?

Do you know anything about any of these organizations? If so, what?

Which organizations might be best for me?

Can you think of others that are not yet on my list?

How do you happen to know that? *(When they have information, this question is to discover the source, which might be a person you should meet, a Web site you should visit, or something you should read.)*

Can you suggest other organizations I should include on my list?

Do you know anyone else who might know more about any of them? If so, would you be comfortable introducing me to them?

Do you know any current or former employees of any them?
If so, would you be comfortable introducing me to that person?

Your goal is to focus on the most suitable organizations, then see what you can do to position yourself for the next appropriate job that comes open. Showing people your Target List is a good way to get them talking about organizations you're interested in.

Naturally, you want to give your resumé to everyone you talk to. However, you don't want the resumé to be the main topic of conversation, so give it to them after you talk with them rather than before.

Give your friends a copy of your Target List as well. And give them a new one from time to time as you revise it. This will remind them to keep their eyes open for information, knowledgeable people, and insiders.

NETWORKING IN THE PIERSON METHOD

1. Show your Target List to friends and acquaintances.
Ask for information about targets.
Get introductions to current employees (insiders) at targeted organizations.

2. Talk to insiders
Find out about the organization and the Decision Maker.
Show them your resumé.
Express interest in working there the next time the right kind of opening happens.
Get an introduction to the Decision Maker if possible.

3. Talk to Decision Makers.
Treat it like an interview, even if it lasts only a few minutes.
Let them know you are interested and qualified.

TALK TO INSIDERS

Your second step is talking to insiders. Sometimes you discover that you already know people inside your target organizations. Naturally, you will not embarrass them by asking them to get you a job. But if you ask the right questions, you can get the information you need to decide whether you want to work there, and if so, how to best position yourself for the next opening. And some of them might actually *want* to help you get a job in their organization, because they like you or consider you a good candidate or both. Some organizations even pay employees a bonus for bringing in a good candidate who is successfully hired.

When talking to insiders, you should consider questions like: What is it like to work there? Which job titles suit you best, and why? What is the pay range for those jobs? Which are the most appropriate departments for you? Exactly what do they do and how? Who are the appropriate Decision Makers? What do they want in employees? Could you meet people in those departments? Could you meet the Decision Maker?

One reason insiders will be happy to talk to you is that you're a good source of information. Because you are in search, you have collected information on their industry, other organizations in that industry, and even on their company. You are also well-informed on career management and happenings in your profession. Many people will be interested in hearing some of this.

TALK TO DECISION MAKERS

Your third step is talking to the Decision Makers themselves, usually before they have an opening. Or at least, before they're ready to admit that they are expecting one. By the time you meet the Decision Maker, you should know something about the organization, what it does, and what kind of people they like to hire and why.

People Hire People

Skills are often used to justify hiring someone the Decision Maker likes or trusts.

Decision Makers can and do hire people who have few of the expected skills.

The reason that this people-talking-to-people technique works so well is that people hire people. While some skills are expected, people do not primarily hire skills. In the end, people often hire people they like, people they share some interest with, and people who are a friend of a friend or an acquaintance of an acquaintance.

Why do they behave like this? Well, it's faster and less expensive than any of the other ways of hiring—as you saw in the hiring scenarios in Chapter 4. But most important, they feel more comfortable that they're getting a good, solid, reliable candidate, because they have talked to someone who knows the person.

The most skilled person does not always get the job, and this is very good news for those of us who are not the top people in our fields. With networking—unlike ads and staffing firms—the resumé often comes last rather than first. You still need one, and it still needs to be appropriate for the organizations you are targeting. But it's not always the most important part of the process.

In Networking, Interest Rules

Expressing a genuine informed interest can overcome a weak resumé.

But you must know enough to be believable.

In networking, your interest is what makes it work. An interested, enthusiastic candidate is highly appealing to Decision Makers. High interest can compensate for low skills. A highly skilled person who is not very interested may not be productive and could easily quit. A highly interested person is likely to get more skilled with every passing day—and be more fun to have around as well.

Interest in the organization is important to insiders and Decision Makers. Members of any organization are pleased when others are interested in it and what it does. If you can answer the question, "Why do you want to work here?" with enthusiasm backed by a real understanding of who they are and what they do, you are automatically a better candidate. This is doubly true if you are at entry level, but it is true for everyone.

Throughout your search, you need to collect information to help you clarify your interests. If you cannot find reasons to be interested in particular jobs or organizations, you should revise your Project Plan to eliminate them. As you find jobs and organizations that interest you, you should let everyone know about your interest.

DON'T NETWORK. JUST TALK TO PEOPLE; HAVE A GOOD TIME

Finally, if you're like me and a little tired of hearing about networking in job search, try this: Forget about networking.

Do your search the easy way. Talk to your family and friends. Start with the ones you're most comfortable with. Some of them actually love you, right? And you love them? Why not start there?

Tell them about your job search. Explain the Pierson Method. See if you can make them comfortable with what you're doing. See if you can be comfortable yourself. Show them your Target List. Discuss the list. See what you can learn.

Ask them if they know anyone familiar with the organizations on your list. Ask who else they know that you can discuss your list with—people who might enjoy meeting you, for any reason. See if together the two of you can find a few people you'd be comfortable talking to. Or might even enjoy.

And proceed like that. If you get stuck or it's not working, it might be good to discuss your search with someone. A Job Search Work Team is a good way to do that. Or maybe you have a person who can be a search coach for you.

Just talk to people. If there's one thing I've learned in my career in career consulting, it is that people talking to people is the way most people find jobs—good jobs. So just talk to people. Do it your way. Have a good time if you can. But do it.

Who knows? It might be good for them as well as you. They might learn something too. They might enjoy talking to you. So just do it.

If you want to know more about networking or any of the seven search techniques, I have recommended some books on them on my Web site, www.highlyeffectivejobsearch.com. In using any of the techniques, you need a way of gauging your progress. That is the topic of the next chapter.

ORVILLE'S JOURNAL

BEN, JESSIE, AND I DISCUSS THE SEVEN SEARCH TECHNIQUES, OR MAYBE JUST THREE

I was back in the rocking chair in the Williams's living room. I had a cup of herbal tea in my hand. Jessie had gone to the kitchen.

"I liked your chapter on the Seven Search Techniques," Ben said. "I'd never heard that there were only seven. I always thought there were more. Me? I would have put the Internet at the top of the list.

"But now I have to agree. Using the Internet in search is way overrated. It's just doing the same old things, only faster. Finding ads. Answering ads. Getting your resumé into the employer's file drawer. But now it's not a drawer, it's a database."

"You're the guest lecturer tonight, Ben?" Jessie asked. She had returned with the biggest tray of assorted cookies I'd ever seen. She set them next to me.

"Yes, he was holding forth on the Internet and job hunting," I volunteered.

"Ah," Jessie said. "Chapter 10. The three search techniques. Well, Ben is something of a Web expert, Orville. Sometimes I think he lives there."

"What do you mean, three techniques?" asked Ben. "There are seven."

"For you, maybe. But I'm not going to do telemarketing, spam, or walk-ins. And the application thing? Not likely. Not me."

"So which of the three is working for you, Jessie?" I asked.

"I actually found some good job listings on the Internet," she replied, "but most of them are too long a commute. Or we'd have to move. I applied for all the local ones, and posted my resumé all over the place. But no results yet. Zero from staffing firms also."

"How many staffing firms have your resumé?" I asked.

"Six," Jessie replied. "But everyone, including my old boss Tom, is telling me that I won't get anything that way. Companies around here don't use staffing firms for my kind of work these days. Too expensive."

"I guess that leaves good old networking, doesn't it?" Ben put in. "Orville hit the nail on the head. Most jobs go through networking."

Jessie looked at him, frowning. "Ben, are you trying out for president of the Orville Pierson Fan Club? That's the second time you've told us how great he is. Want him to get a swollen head? Orville," she said, turning to me, "can we get back to Chapter 10?"

"Sure," I said. "I don't need a fan club, I've got cookies. You've been using networking?"

"It got me two interviews and one offer, didn't it?" Jessie replied. "But I don't like the name networking. It sounds kind of fake to me. Reminds me of network marketing. Network parties. Computer networks. And all that other—"

"But you're doing it, hon," Ben interrupted. "You're doing a good job. And it's working."

"Yes," she said. "Yes it is. Thanks to Judy, I got connected to a whole bunch of teachers in just a few days. I'm going to stay in touch with them, since I've got a career change on the calendar in five years.

"And Tom. Tom's been so helpful ...

"And Francine! Francine's going to talk to me! I almost forgot to tell you, Orville. I sent her an e-mail. She called and asked me to stop by. I know nothing's happening at Western, but she's got some ideas for me. And maybe even some introductions."

"That's great." I said. "And who else?"

"I don't really know," Jessie said. "Those three were really great. But now I'm kind of stuck. I don't know anyone else."

"You have lots more, Jess," Ben offered, "and any one of them might be as good as Judy, Tom, and Francine. You just don't know what will happen until you try them. There's George James, the Goldsteins, Frieda Nicholson, Jack at my office, Cindy, Laura, Keisha, Anne—and that's not counting the list you made."

"You're right, Ben. I've been looking for higher-ups like Tom and Francine," Jessie said. "I just need to get going again, talking to friends—people like Judy—and see what happens. I'm actually looking forward to talking to Keisha and Laura. I should have told them about my search a long time ago."

"So you're going to start using that list," I suggested, "and Ben's going to help you add names if you need more?"

They both smiled and nodded.

Good heavens, I thought, now I'm giving out work assignments. And no one is objecting.

"Yes," said Jessie, "and I'm going to keep better records on who I talk to. What information I get, and all that."

"And she's using the Progress Chart," Ben volunteered.

"You can't talk about that yet," Jessie admonished him. "That's Chapter 11."

QUESTION:	**Before you have interviews or offers, how do you know if you're making progress in your search?**

ANSWER:	You keep score by tracking how many of each of these you rack up each week: **Hours** you spend on job search. **Letters** you write and mail or e-mail. **Conversations** you have in person or on the phone with anyone about your job search. **Conversations you have with Decision Makers** in targeted organizations.

CHAPTER ELEVEN

Keeping Score

For many years I have looked at job hunters the way a coach might look at athletes. Some job hunters are superstars from the start. They get going quickly, learn new ways of doing things, work hard, and usually know what needs to be done. They have a strong sense of what is important in the search project and what's not. They ask me questions—good questions—about the best ways to proceed. Then they make the advice their own and put it into action immediately.

Then there are the job hunters who don't have a clue. They feel overwhelmed by the job of job hunting. They don't know what to do or when or how to do it. They are affected by all the barriers that we discussed in Chapter 3 and can't seem to get around them. Left to their own devices, they do very little effective work each week, sometimes putting most of their time into tasks not likely to produce results.

Of course, the majority of job hunters fit in somewhere between these two extreme groups. As a job hunting program designer, it's my job to find ways to teach all job hunters how to do the job better. I figured I'd take the same approach that I would if I were coaching a basketball team.

If I coached basketball, I'd look at some of the top players in the game—Michael Jordan, Shaquille O'Neal, Tim Duncan, and Jason

Kidd, maybe. Then I'd see if I could teach my players to be a little more like them. Naturally, you can't teach everyone to be a star, but if you can teach them to imitate just a few of the good things the top players do, they'd improve enough to win.

Luckily for me, job hunting is much easier than basketball. It isn't difficult to see the differences between the top job hunters and the least effective ones. For starters, the top ones do more work every week. They talk to more people. They read more. They meet more insiders. They're willing to try new approaches. They learn more. They talk to more Decision Makers.

So what I did was identify some key areas of effort that could be numerically measured. Then I measured job hunters with these simple measuring rods. I compared those who found jobs quickly with those who took a longer time to land one.

Sure enough, there were large differences between what the quick landers did every week and what the slower job hunters did. So I started teaching everyone how to keep score in job search, and also how to play the game more like the star performers, so they can rack up more points more quickly.

KEEPING SCORE

In sports like basketball and football, the team with the highest score wins, so the players are trying to score as many points as possible while keeping the opponent from scoring points. In bowling, the perfect score is 300, so whether you are playing against others or not, you would certainly like to get to 300.

People also have ways of keeping score in various work projects. If you needed to nail down 30 sheets of plywood to complete the subfloor of a new house, you would be halfway done after 15. If you were writing a 300-page book, you would be two-thirds done when you got to page 200.

KEEPING SCORE IN JOB SEARCH

As we saw in Chapter 4, the most important scorekeeping in job search is counting the number of different Decision Makers you have talked to.

As we've mentioned, the rule of thumb is that it takes conversations with 25 different Decision Makers—in an appropriate Target Market—to get a job. The number might be a bit higher if your personal job market is flooded with candidates. Or a bit lower if your qualifications are particularly good.

The number 25 is an average. Some people will be hired by the first Decision Maker they talk to. Others will need to talk to more than 25, even though they are well qualified and have a good Project Plan. These are not interviews; they are simply conversations. On the phone or in person. Sometimes lasting an hour or more and sometimes only a few minutes.

Most people underestimate the number needed. They get discouraged if the first Decision Maker doesn't hire them. This is like scoring 32 in bowling and wondering why you didn't win. Or thinking your book is done after writing 10 pages. You need to stay with it and keep working on it.

You need to get your numbers up. You can learn to do that. Like anything in life, it takes some experimentation and practice.

COUNTING HOURS, E-MAILS, LETTERS, AND OTHER CONVERSATIONS

Beyond Decision Makers, there are other useful measures of progress in search: the hours you spend in various search activities, the number of letters and e-mails you send, and conversations with people other than Decision Makers. On the following pages we will look at each. Let's start with the simplest one: hours.

Tracking Your Hours

Total number of hours per week you spend on:

Education and planning

Research

Letter writing

Administration

Talking to people on the phone and in person

The easiest place to start measuring your progress is counting the hours. As a rule of thumb, 25 to 35 hours a week is about right if you are unemployed. Search can be stressful; 50 hours may not be a good idea. For someone employed while doing a job search, five to 10 hours a week is good. But consistent effort is necessary, week after week. Nothing happens in any work project without effort over time, and search is no exception.

The next question is: What *kind* of effort are you making? How many hours are you putting into what kind of activity? After all, some activities are more likely to produce results.

At the beginning of your search project, education and planning are important, and you might spend all of your time on those for a week or more—reading this book, for instance, and creating a Project Plan. But once your search is under way, education and planning are not necessary every week.

Listing your targets and collecting information on them might also occupy a lot of your time at the outset. But after you've researched an initial Target List, your library and Internet time should drop to perhaps 10 percent of your weekly search time for the rest of your search.

Sending letters and e-mails is inevitable in a search project, but this written communication should usually be to set up telephone or in-person conversations and to follow up afterward. Once again, you may do more writing at the outset, when you're testing ads and staffing firms. You will soon develop standard sentences, paragraphs, and letters for routine uses like ads. Once you're under way, this activity should also be about 10 percent of your weekly time—or less.

Administration is the business of keeping track of what you've done, whom you have talked to, and what you've said to whom. While you may need to put some energy into setting up tracking systems at the beginning, time here should quickly drop to 5 percent or less.

TALKING TO PEOPLE

Please notice that all of these activities so far—education, research, writing, and administration—are introverted activities. If you are a natural introvert, that works very well with many jobs and is consistent with much of the initial work of the search project. On the other hand, extroverts may need to make an extra effort on seeing that their preparation is thoroughly done before they get on the phone.

But once your search is established, the Pierson Method suggests that you spend most of your time—about 75 percent—talking to people, whether you're introverted or extroverted.

Even for those lucky people who get interviews through ads and staffing agencies, talking to a wide range of other people is important to develop the information necessary to evaluate organizations and offers. Most of the best information in job search is developed by talking to people, and doing some of that before your first interview comes along is very useful.

Tracking Your Letters

Total number of letters you mailed or e-mailed each week, including:

Direct mail

Advertised positions

Staffing firms (including search firms)

Other letters

When it comes to job search, many people think only of written communication—sending out resumés, cover letters, and e-mails, or completing applications. While not the most important part of search, sending letters and e-mails is necessary and needs to be tracked.

The most important written communication might be sending resumés to ads and staffing firms, two of the more productive of the Seven Search Techniques. With ads on the Internet or in print, the average candidate might send 50 cover letters and resumés to get one interview. If you get up to 75 with no invitations to interview, you should certainly recheck your Project Plan and probably redo your resumé.

With executive search firms, if 50 to 100 appropriate firms have your best possible resumé and no one invites you to an interview, it might be time to conclude that this is not the best avenue for you. I'm not saying to give up on it completely, but it is probably not the best place to spend a lot of time. Or maybe you need to do a complete resumé makeover and try again.

Direct mail, or sending letters with or without resumés to total strangers—people who have never heard of you—is not productive for most people, but should nonetheless be tracked. In this category, the average person needs to send over 1,000 (yes, one thousand) resumés to total strangers in order to get one interview. In direct mail, these are people who have not placed an ad, have never heard of you, and with whom you have no connection whatsoever. If you know them or have a referral, it's not direct mail—it's networking.

"Other letters" are mostly follow-up letters and e-mails to people you have already spoken with. These are a very important part of your search, since the combination of telephone, letters, e-mails, and personal meetings is how you move your networking along.

Tracking Your Contacts

Total number of job search conversations you have each week (on the phone or in person) with:

General Network contacts

Target organization miscellaneous contacts

Target organization peer contacts

Decision Maker and contacts above Decision Maker
Follow-up with Decision Makers

When I use the word "contacts," I am not talking about senators, CEOs of businesses, or leaders in your industry or community. If you are friends with this kind of person, that's great, and you will certainly include them in your search. But for anyone in search, "contact" simply means reaching out and making contact with other human beings. And talking to them.

JOB SEARCH CONVERSATIONS

Since talking to people about your job search is the most productive thing you can do, counting those conversations is your most important progress measurement. Decision Maker conversations are central, but conversations with all kinds of other people are also very important in gathering information on your chosen Target Market and in getting the opportunity to talk to Decision Makers.

There are two kinds of contacts in job search: insiders, or people who are employed in organizations where you might want to work; and outsiders, or people who are not. In the Pierson Method, we call the second group "General Network" contacts. You might think that those who are not employed in your targets are less important. This isn't always true. They could be your most important contacts, and you won't know until you talk to them about your Target List.

The Benefits of General Network Contacts
Information on your targets
The names of new targets
Introductions to new General Network contacts
Introductions to insiders in targeted organizations

Your General Network contacts are a huge asset for two reasons. First, they're easy for you to talk to, since they are friends, relatives, friends of friends, members of groups you belong to (social, religious, educational, political, former employers, or any other), and other people you have a connection with. Second, they have a wealth of information that they're usually more than willing to share, if you know how to ask the right questions.

Your Target List is the key to success in talking to this group of people, since it will focus the conversation on what they know about the listed organizations (and others like them). They may know people who know even more about those organizations. They may be able to introduce you to insiders, and even Decision Makers. The best starting point for these conversations is talking about the Pierson Method, your Project Plan, or your Target List.

While you may sometimes strike it rich and talk to a General Network contact who introduces you directly to a Decision Maker or someone even higher, the most common successes are smaller steps: getting information on targets, getting the names of good new targets, getting introduced to other General Network contacts, and getting introduced to insiders below the Decision Maker level.

The Benefits of Peer and Miscellaneous Contacts

Information about the organization, jobs, and the Decision Maker
An introduction to the Decision Maker

Talking to people at your own level inside targeted organizations is nearly as valuable as talking to Decision Makers. These insiders in the department where you want to work know everything you need to know—especially if they now hold the job title you're interested in. They can tell you about the job and what it takes to succeed in it. They can tell you about the organization, what it's like to work there, and what the pay ranges are.

All of this will help you decide if this is a place where you want to work. If you don't like the people who would be your peers and coworkers, you should probably cross the organization off your Target List.

Peers can also tell you about their boss, who is your Decision Maker and possibly your future boss. They can tell you what that person wants in employees, what they like and dislike generally, and the best ways to approach them. They might be willing to introduce you to the boss.

Even if you had the opportunity to talk to the Decision Maker on your own, you'd be better off talking to peer contacts first. Doing it that way, you're more likely to say the right thing when you talk to the Decision Maker.

As we noticed in Chapter 4, employees may be asked by the boss for the names of job candidates, and sometimes even paid a bonus for providing candidates. Some job hunters succeed in search simply by talking to a lot of peers in a number of different targets. Then one day the Decision Maker (who heard about them from one of their peer contacts) calls them and invites them for an interview.

MISCELLANEOUS CONTACTS IN TARGET ORGANIZATIONS

If you can't locate a peer, you can start by talking to someone below your level inside of a target organization. Any insider knows things you do not, and any insider may be able to introduce you to someone in the right department. Anyone in the organization may be able to introduce you to a peer or even a Decision Maker.

THE CHAIN OF INTRODUCTIONS

Successful job hunters usually have about 15 conversations with non–Decision Makers for each conversation with a Decision Maker. When the job hunter asks the right questions, some of those 15 conversations will produce introductions to the next link in the chain that leads to the right Decision Maker.

Usually the chain of introductions begins with your talking to a friend about your Target List. That person knows people who have information on your targets and introduces you. Those "second level" people introduce you to insiders currently employed at your targets.

One of those insiders introduces you to the Decision Maker. Sometimes you're lucky and skip some links in the chain. Nearly always—if you are asking the right questions—you learn things along the way that move your search forward.

There are two very important things to remember about making this chain happen. One is that everyone has to be comfortable with the introductions. Some of your initial contacts will be comfortable introducing you to everyone they know. Some will not. You want your contacts to play matchmaker and introduce you only to those people they think you are compatible with—people you might like and who might like you. That way everyone is happy.

And the second thing you need to remember is to always ask for introductions. When an appropriate person is mentioned in conversation, your next line is, "Would you be comfortable introducing me to them?"

CONTACTING DECISION MAKERS AND FOLLOWING UP WITH THEM

You remember, of course, that the average search by the average candidate requires conversations with 25 different Decision Makers. The Decision Maker is your next boss, or your boss's boss. These conversations can be on the phone or in person. Initial conversations with Decision Makers might only be a few minutes, since the formal interview does not come until the Decision Maker is ready to announce that there is an opening.

About 20 percent—or one in five—of your conversations with Decision Makers should be very serious. This could mean a formal job interview in which you are one of a small number being considered for an actual opening. Or it could be a longer informal conversation in which the Decision Maker clearly lets you know that you are the kind of candidate they like to hire when they have a need—or makes some other clear expression of interest in you.

This means that the average candidate comes close to being hired by five of the 25 Decision Makers they talk to in their search. Sometimes those close calls are more difficult to deal with than rejection or lack of interest. You get your hopes up. Possibly way up. Then it doesn't work out. This happens four or five times in the average search.

But job search is a numbers game, and if you remember that and track your numbers, it will help you weather the disappointments and keep going.

Many Decision Maker conversations are simply to say "Hello," mention your interest in the organization, and use your two-minute statement about yourself if you get the chance. If you're lucky enough to get a longer conversation, treat it like an informal job interview— find out what the Decision Maker expects from employees and tell them how you have some (or all) of what they're looking for. Get acquainted. Tell them you would be very interested in talking to them the next time they have an opening. Leave your resumé if possible.

If you get the chance to talk to someone above the Decision Maker— your next boss's boss, in other words—you should certainly do that. You should also exercise the same caution and courtesy that you always exercise when talking to your boss's boss. In the Pierson Method, we count these conversations along with Decision Maker conversations. When we say it takes 25 Decision Makers, we mean both of them together.

Once you have talked to a Decision Maker, you need to follow up on a regular basis—every two to four weeks. This is one of the most neglected aspects of job search. Those who do it succeed more quickly and easily than those who do not.

These follow-up contacts do not need to be long conversations. They can be mail, e-mail, telephone, or in person. The point is to let the Decision Maker know that you are still available and still very interested in their organization. Doing this is what keeps you on the Decision Maker's mental short list, so they'll remember you the next time they need someone.

Because these follow-up conversations are so important, you need to count them separately. This also allows you to keep an accurate count of the total number of *different* Decision Makers you have talked to— the number that you are working to get up to 25.

Progress Chart

DATE (week of)								
Job Search Education								
Research								
Letters and Admin.								
Network: phone								
Network: In person								
TOTAL HOURS								
Direct mail								
Advertised positions								
Search Firms								
Other Letters								
TOTAL LETTERS								
General network (include search firms)								
Target company Miscellaneous. contact								
Target company Peer contact								
Target company Decision Maker/above								
Follow-ups with Decision Maker/above								
TOTAL CONTACTS								

A full- size version of this chart can be downloaded free
from www.highlyeffectivejobsearch.com

TRACK YOUR PROGRESS WITH THE PROGRESS CHART

Along with the Project Plan, the Progress Chart is one of your most important search management tools. Shown on the facing page (a larger downloadable version is available at www.highlyeffectivejobsearch.com), it is a simple way of gauging your progress in search.

Each column represents seven days, one week, in search. Each week, you write the number of hours you worked on search in the top section, the number of written communications (letters, notes, or e-mails, but referred to in the chart as "letters") you sent out in the middle section, and the number of job search conversations you had in the bottom section.

The bottom section is the most important. Talking to a lot of people is much more important than putting in hours. If you are unemployed and had 30 search-related conversations in a week, you had a good week. If you did that in 20 hours instead of 35, that's even better. If you are conducting a search while employed and had 10 search-related conversations in a week, that's very good.

WHERE'S THE LINE FOR INTERVIEWS?

The Progress Chart has no row for counting interviews. There are two reasons for this. The first reason is very simple: You can't control whether you get an interview or not. When you're in job search, you need to stay productive every week, doing things that will move your search ahead. You need to hold yourself accountable for putting some numbers on the chart every week. But you can't hold yourself accountable for interviews, because that's decided by the Decision Maker, not you.

Here's the other reason there's no interview line: When you're using the Pierson Method, you can never quite be sure what was an interview and what was not. Suppose you talk to a Decision Maker today and that person does not admit to having a job opening now or in the foreseeable future. That's not an interview, because an interview is when the two of you are talking about your qualifications to fill an opening.

Now suppose that the same Decision Maker calls you next week and tells you there's an opening. You go in to talk about it. Is that your second interview or your first? The first conversation can become an interview later, when there's an opening. At the time you had it, however, it was just a friendly talk.

So you might want to separately count how many Decision Maker conversations later turn into interviews. Just like you might want to track your hit rate on advertised jobs. But on the chart, we only count what you can control.

GIVE YOURSELF CREDIT

Many people using the Progress Chart undercount their search conversations, not giving themselves enough credit for what they accomplished. In the Pierson Method, you should be counting *all* search conversations—not just the ones you thought went well. Sometimes the one you thought went badly is the one where the other person later gives your name to the Decision Maker.

If you talk to your spouse or best friend about your search, showing them your Project Plan and asking for information about specific targets, that counts as a General Network conversation. If you have an inside contact at a target organization and have reason to talk to them twice in one week, that counts as two Target Peer conversations. You can and should talk to some people repeatedly—once or even twice a week—throughout your search.

It's great when the conversation results in useful information or in introductions to other people. But all search-related conversations count, whether they produce immediate results or not, and whether or not you were happy about how they went.

Progress Chart Samples

Slower Search	
DATE (week of)	8/5
Job Search Education	5
Research	8
Letters and Admin.	2
Network: phone	9
Network: In person	6
TOTAL HOURS	**30**
Direct mail	0
Advertised positions	*
Search Firms	**
Other Letters	6
TOTAL LETTERS	**6**
General network (include search firms)	11
Target company Miscellaneous contact	2
Target company Peer contact	1
Target company Decision Maker/above	1
Follow-ups with Decision Maker/above	0
TOTAL CONTACTS	**15**

Faster Search	
DATE (week of)	2/3
Job Search Education	2
Research	3
Letters and Admin.	4
Network: phone	14
Network: In person	7
TOTAL HOURS	**30**
Direct mail	5
Advertised positions	*
Search Firms	**
Other Letters	15
TOTAL LETTERS	**20**
General network (include search firms)	23
Target company Miscellaneous. contact	2
Target company Peer contact	3
Target company Decision Maker/above	2
Follow-ups with Decision Maker/above	4
TOTAL CONTACTS	**34**

*Advertised positions: as many as you can find
**Search Firms: up to 100 for the entire search
Follow-up, Decision Makers: goes up as the search progresses

A Good Week in Search

25 to 35 hours

15 to 30 total contacts

One or two new Decision Makers

Follow-up contact with Decision Makers

Five to 50 letters, notes, and e-mails

The chart on page 217 shows what numbers might look like in an average week in search for someone moving quickly and for someone moving more slowly. Both of these are unemployed people. Employed people are doing well if their numbers are 25 to 33 percent of those shown.

If your full-time search is moving even more slowly than the lower numbers, it might be a good idea to get some help—by reading more books on job search, by talking to someone who knows how to do it, or by joining or starting a Job Search Work Team (see the Special Section, "Team Up for a Successful Search").

People usually have some zeros on their Progress Chart. Zeros in Direct Mail might be a good thing, if you're talking to people. Some people simply find no relevant ads and always have zeros in that row. Many people try a lot of staffing firms early in their search and discover that those firms simply cannot do anything for them. Then they have zeros in that row for the rest of their search.

But the most important thing in search is to have numbers above zero somewhere on the chart every week. And to do a little bit better each week than you did last week. If the phone seems to weigh 100 pounds this week and you're having a great deal of trouble picking it up, send out some e-mails with your Target List to good friends. Ask them some questions in the e-mail and ask them to phone you when they have read it.

That way, you'll have some numbers in the letters row this week, and maybe some in the General Network row next week when your friends call. And maybe the phone will be lighter next week. Then you can call some of those people you sent e-mails to this week.

MAKING PROGRESS

Before you have a job offer—or even an interview—your Progress Chart will tell you that you are making progress, and approximately how much progress you're making. The more Decision Maker conversations you've had, the more likely that one of them will call you in for an interview—especially if you have some numbers in the Follow-up row.

Even if your total numbers in the Decision Maker row are a long way from 25, contacts you have made with insiders, either Peer or Miscellaneous, can also result in a call from a Decision Maker. And who knows who your General Network contacts might talk to about you?

So get some numbers on your chart. And each week, try to increase them a bit. Finding a great new job slowly is almost as good as finding one quickly. You only need one Decision Maker to decide to hire you, and you don't know when or how that will happen. The key person could be the next person you talk to. So keep moving. Keep your numbers up. You will get there.

The Progress Chart is the last element of the Pierson Method. The next chapter summarizes the entire method.

ORVILLE'S JOURNAL

JESSIE AND BEN BOTH CONFESS, AND I FINALLY GET BEYOND COOKIES

It had been two weeks since Jessie, Ben, and I had last talked. Now we were meeting in my living room, since I figured it was my turn to supply the refreshments. Chips and dips.

"I have a confession to make," Jessie said.

"Jessica," I said, looking at her sternly over my reading glasses, "just don't tell me you've slacked off again because you had a good talk with a Decision Maker, or you'll be in big trouble."

"No, it's not that. What I want to confess is that I finished reading your book a long time ago. I've just been pretending to do this one-chapter-at-a-time thing."

"Me too," Ben put in. "I finished it before she did. Jess was reading slower back when she was mad about how slow her search was going."

I shrugged. "Well, I don't know what there is to confess. The two of you both talk about the wrong chapter just about every time we get together. So tell me, Jessie, how long have you been using the Progress Chart?"

"Several weeks," she replied, "but I'm still below two Decision Makers a week."

"That's perfectly normal," I said. "It takes a while to get the hang of it. And get some things in the pipeline. You need to talk to a bunch of other people to meet Decision Makers."

"She's sure doing that," Ben said. "Our phone bill is going up. She's calling people all over the country."

"That's great," I said. "Sometimes out-of-town people can give you great information. Makes a local search go better."

Jessie agreed. "Some of that's happening. But Ben's exaggerating. Most of my calls are local. I'm spending a lot more money taking people to lunch than I am on phone bills."

"That's also a good thing," I said, "if you can afford it."

"I don't think she can afford not to," Ben put in. "Anyway, it's a good investment. Last time I looked for a job, that's what I did."

"Back in those days," Jessie said, "lunch was two bucks and coffee was 50 cents. But I agree, it's a good investment. I'm looking to do it three times a week. My General Network contacts were up to 22 last week—mostly on the phone."

"Twenty-two! That's great!" I exclaimed. "Any insiders?"

"Three last week, at three different organizations," Jessie answered, "All peers, more or less."

"Watch out." I said. "Keep that up and we won't be having these soirees. You'll be working. And you'll owe me dinner."

Jessie smiled. "Yup."

"I have a question," Ben said. "Do e-mails count as conversations with contacts? I use e-mails all the time, and have since coffee was a buck fifty."

"Here's my rule of thumb," I replied. "If it goes back and forth three times, it can be counted as one conversation. Otherwise, it's a letter. Are you still supervising Jessie's search?"

Ben smiled. "No, I'm planning my next one. I like to get things figured out well in advance."

Jessie reached for some chips. "Orville, am I allowed to talk about the Special Section? The one on Job Search Work Teams? I know this is supposed be about Chapter 11, but I have a question on teams."

"Sure," I replied, "now that you've confessed, why not?"

"Well, I've been finding these meetings with you and Ben very helpful. Now that we're almost through with all the chapters, can we make our meetings into Job Search Work Team meetings? We could meet at my house, and I'd supply the refreshments. I'd like to have my own little team. Officially."

"I'd get free cookies every week?"

"Yes. Lots of them. Huge trays of them."

"I accept."

"There's actually another reason I want to do it,' Jessie continued, "Ben and I are thinking about using the Job Search Work Teams in our church jobs program. That's why Ben's been asking all those questions. Besides liking to look smart and boss me around. We want to try it." Ben nodded his agreement.

"Sounds good," I said. "When do we start?"

"How about a week from today, same time?"

As it turned out, we didn't have many meetings. Jessie did beat the odds. She found a job with only 11 Decision Maker conversations. The next thing I knew, I had gone from free cookies to a free dinner.

That's how it is for us career consultants sometimes. Our clients work really hard and get new jobs. Then we get free dinner.

The Pierson Method

1	**GET READY: Plan and prepare** Read this book. Create a Project Plan, Target List, and resumé.
2	**GET MOVING: Take a systematic approach.** Gather information, talk to people, and follow up. Use the Seven Search Techniques.
3	**MANAGE YOUR SEARCH: Use progress measurements** Track your progress and check your Project Plan regularly. Interview, negotiate, and start your new job.

CHAPTER TWELVE

The Pierson Method

In Chapter 11, I told you about how I created the Pierson Method by observing how the best job hunters work on their search projects. In addition to observing the best, I also observed people less effective in search: many good people struggling with their job hunting and having a terrible time of it.

Most people are lucky enough not to have to go job hunting more than 10 or 15 times in their life, so they don't get a lot of experience in it. In addition, they are sometimes misled by books and articles written by people with limited experience in career work. So when they have to do a search, they make mistakes and don't always do it very well.

Over the years, I watched the problems and difficulties people had in job search. The Pierson Method is designed to help you avoid all of the most common problems. I've listed these on page 226, and as you read them you will notice (I hope) that you now know how to avoid all of them. If not, look at the list at the bottom of the page and it will tell you where to find the antidote to each problem. You can also visit www.highlyeffectivejobsearch.com for additional information and ideas.

The 10 Top Reasons Why It Takes People Too Long to Find a Job

1. They don't put much time or effort into job hunting.

2. They waste time on unproductive activities.

3. They have no way of measuring their progress.

4. They're not sure what kind of work they're looking for.

5. They don't make a list of prospective employers—or it's not long enough.

6. They don't define and analyze their own personal job market.

7. They have no systematic approach to the job search project.

8. They only pursue announced job openings and use no proactive approaches.

9. They don't realize that search is a numbers game—or they seriously underestimate the numbers needed.

10. They go it alone, without any objective advice or support.

If you've read the last 11 chapters, you now know how to avoid all of these problems.

Here is where you can find information on the above items:

1. Chapter 3
2. The entire book
3. Chapter 11
4. Chapter 6
5. Chapter 7
6. Chapters 5, 6, 7, 8, and 9
7. The entire Pierson Method
8. Chapter 4 and the entire book
9. Chapters 9, 11, and the entire book
10. The Special Section on Job Search Work Teams

This chapter is a summary of the entire book. It summarizes how you can imitate the best job hunters and avoid the worst pitfalls. It is a road map to success in search. I have listed all 12 steps of the Pierson Method and told you exactly what needs to be done in search, repeating the key points in the book and adding a new one here and there. Each step also has chapter references, so you can go back and review the relevant sections of the book if you would like to.

The 12 steps of the Pierson Method fall into three phases:

Get Ready: Plan and prepare

Get Moving: Take a systematic approach

Manage Your Search: Use progress measurements.

GET READY

Preparation, or getting ready, starts with understanding the search process. If you have read the preceding 11 chapters, you have a great start at this preparation and have already completed the first step in a successful search. Creating a Project Plan and Target List are the most important preparations. Once those are in place, you are ready to write an outstanding resumé based on them.

GET MOVING

Getting your search moving is all about talking to people, some inside targeted organizations and some not. Gathering information is the immediate goal of these conversations. Of course, you are always looking to get introduced to insiders, especially Decision Makers. And usually before they have an opening. Those introductions most often happen because you are talking to a lot of people about your Target List and asking the right questions.

This sequence of events is what most often happens in effective networking. For about 25 percent of job hunters, one of the other six of the Seven Search Techniques is the route to the Decision Maker. But talking to people can make the other six techniques work better too.

MANAGE YOUR SEARCH

While using any of the Seven Search Techniques, you must manage your search. The two most important ways to do this are using the Progress Chart and refining your Project Plan if there is a need to do so. Sooner or later your steady job search work will take you to interviewing, negotiating, and starting a new job.

In the remainder of this chapter we'll go through the 12 steps of the Pierson Method, with a summary of each step.

Get Ready

STEP 1: READ *THE UNWRITTEN RULES OF THE HIGHLY EFFECTIVE JOB SEARCH*

Whether you read this entire book or just the large headings and summaries, you need to have a clear picture of how hiring is done and the best ways to plan and manage a search. This overview of the entire project is very important. It lets you keep the day-to-day details of the search in perspective.

STEP 2: CREATE A PROJECT PLAN AND TARGET LIST

Your Project Plan should consist of three parts:

1. **Professional Objective.** What kind of work do you want to do? Write this in three sentences or less. Give several sample job titles (see Chapter 6).

2. **Target Market.** Which organizations do you want to work for? Write out the exact geographic area(s) in which you will conduct your search, the industries or types of organizations you are most

interested in, and the size range of the organizations (see Chapter 7). Use these criteria to create a Target List of organizations (Chapter 7).

3. **Core Message.** What will you say about yourself to Decision Makers in your Target Market? Write an outline (about half a page) of the Core Message about yourself you want everyone to know. It should tell your Target Market why you're good at the kinds of work described by your Professional Objective (see Chapter 8). Then use that outline to create a two-minute verbal summary of why you're a good candidate for the jobs in your Professional Objective.

STEP 3: DO A REALITY-CHECK ON YOUR PROJECT PLAN

Do a Reality Check on your Project Plan to make sure there will be enough organizations on your Target List and enough openings happening over the course of your search (see Chapter 9). In addition to doing numerical estimates, talk to several people who know your field to make sure you are qualified for your Professional Objective. These people could be current or former Decision Makers, current or former employees, or simply people familiar with that kind of work. These same people may be able to tell you what to emphasize on your resumé.

STEP 4: WRITE YOUR RESUMÉ

Your resumé should transmit your Core Message (from Step 2) to your Target Market. People usually want to write their resumé first, as the first step. But you'll write a much better resumé after you have a Project Plan, since you will be clearer on what you need to say and who you are talking to. Be sure to include accomplishments in your resumé (see Chapter 8). If you want to know where to get more information on resumé writing, go to my Web site, www.highlyeffectivejobsearch.com.

Get Moving

STEP 5: GATHER INFORMATION ON YOUR TARGETS

Check the Web sites of each of your top targets and read anything else you can find about them. Your best information will always come from current and former employees, and from people with experience dealing with the organization. Prepare a list of questions to ask about these organizations (NOT including whether they are currently hiring). Show your Project Plan and Target List to friends and acquaintances. Ask them questions (see Chapter 10).

STEP 6: TALK TO INSIDERS, DECISION MAKERS, AND EVERYONE ELSE

Let anyone inside target organizations—including Decision Makers—know how interested you are. Be sure to tell them why you believe you would be a good candidate the next time they have an opening. Give them a resumé, or follow up with one.

With people not inside target organizations, show them your Project Plan and Target List and ask for information about any possible target organization, whether it is on your list or not. Explain how you are conducting your search. Always ask if they can introduce you to anyone else, especially insiders at your targets—and, of course, Decision Makers (see Chapter 10).

With anyone you talk to, consider including a statement like this: "I am looking for a new job. I am particularly interested in (Professional Objective), because that kind of work fits well with my background in (use your Core Message) and with organizations like (mention some sample targets)." Give them your resumé and Target List at the end of the conversation, or send it to them soon afterward. Ask them to keep an eye out for information about any targets.

STEP 7: FOLLOW UP REGULARLY

Every two to four weeks recontact each of the Decision Makers you have met or talked to before. Always make any expressions of interest that you can honestly make. If you have come across any information (articles, Web sites, or people) that might be of interest to them, pass that on. Don't forget to tell them how interested you are.

You should also follow up with everyone that you talk to, including friends and acquaintances. Usually the best follow-up with people in this category is simply to tell them what has happened since you last talked to them. If you talked to a person whom they referred you to, tell them about that. If you have added new targets to your Target List, you might want to talk about these, and to give the contact an updated list.

Follow-up, especially with Decision Makers, is often neglected in search. Those who do it find new jobs faster. People often worry about being a nuisance by regularly recontacting Decision Makers. But Decision Makers must know about your interest, and if you fail to follow up, you have proven that you're not very interested. Find a polite way of following up, a helpful way, if possible. But don't overlook it. The way I see it, you have everything to gain and nothing to lose.

STEP 8: TEST THE SEVEN SEARCH TECHNIQUES

Everyone in search should consider using all of the Seven Search Techniques (see Chapter 10). You may find that you can eliminate the use of some of them quickly, but please do consider all of them. Even if you rarely use some of them, there may be a time or two when they fit. You may need to experiment with some—agencies or recruiters, for example—to see if they work for you. If they result in conversations with Decision Makers, they are certainly worth spending more time on.

Direct Mail is a technique you can do a little bit of now and then when you cannot find anything better to do in your search. Send out some resumés to targets where you haven't met any insiders yet. It's much better than buying lottery tickets. And you might get a callback. You never know.

Everyone must use at least one of these seven techniques. Networking is the one most likely to work for most people. If you want to read more about any of these techniques, the Web site www.highly-effectivejobsearch.com has recommendations on books.

Manage Your Search

STEP 9: TRACK YOUR PROGRESS EACH WEEK

Use the Progress Chart in Chapter 11 to track your progress weekly. Check your progress against the suggestions in the sample Progress Charts on page 217. Join or create a Job Search Work Team if possible (see the Special Section on Job Search Work Teams, following this chapter).

Below is what a good week in search might look like, if you're unemployed. If you're employed, a quarter to a third of this activity level is good.

25 to 35 hours
15 to 30 total contacts
One or two new Decision Makers
Follow up contact with Decision Makers
Five to 50 letters, notes, and e-mails

STEP 10: CHECK YOUR PROJECT PLAN REGULARLY

You should always look for evidence that your Project Plan is working. The best evidence is interviews. Second best is Decision Makers saying that you're the kind of person they like to hire or even expressing a willingness to do that when an opportunity arises. Positive feedback on your qualifications from any insiders in your target organizations is also good evidence you're on the right track. If you get strong positive feedback from the Decision Maker or get an actual interview in 20 percent or more of your Decision Maker contacts, it's a very good sign that your Project Plan is working.

If you've been in active search for a month or more and have not found any evidence that your Project Plan is right for you, you need to find out what the problem is. It could be that you need to improve your Project Plan. Or it could be a problem in how you are using the Seven Search Techniques. If possible, discuss it with someone. This is another place where a Job Search Work Team can help.

STEP 11: INTERVIEW

An interview is a discussion with a Decision Maker who has a current or upcoming job opening and sees you as a candidate for it. Since these formal interviews do not happen often and are hard to get, preparing for the interview and for the negotiations that might follow is important. Even though this is listed as Step 11, you can begin preparing sooner. Again, www.highlyeffectivejobsearch.com has recommendations on books on interviewing.

Some of this preparation should be done well in advance: preparing for commonly asked questions, practicing in mock interview sessions with friends or Job Search Work Team teammates, and collecting information (including salary information) as you network. When an interview is scheduled, visit the Web site of the organization and do an Internet search on them as well. If possible, get a day or two to think over an offer and consult with a knowledgeable person about it—and the possibility of negotiating to improve it.

STEP 12: START YOUR NEW JOB AND DO WELL IN IT

Be sure to talk to your new boss (formerly called the Decision Maker) when you start your new job to confirm their expectations of you. Check in frequently over the first 90 days to make sure you are meeting their expectations, and if not, find out exactly what you need to do differently, and do it. As you get established, reduce the frequency—but it is still a good habit, and one that can help you avoid surprises at your annual performance review.

Using the Pierson Method While Employed

People who are employed while conducting a search for a better job need to be more careful in some of the steps. It is often true that if an employer thinks you're planning to leave, they will have fewer qualms about letting you go. You might rise to the top of the layoff list, if there is one.

DO NOT LEAVE YOUR OLD JOB UNTIL YOU HAVE A NEW ONE

It is usually best not to plan to leave until you have a starting date for your new job. Then give reasonable notice and leave. Before that, if someone discovers that you have sent out some resumés or had an interview, the best response is probably, "I've been told that it is good career management to send out resumés from time to time to test the market, and I have always done a bit of that. But I certainly have no plans to leave." After all, until you have a new job, you do plan to stay, and do not plan to leave. If you can honestly do so, add some comments about liking your current job or organization.

Before starting a job search while employed, make sure you've exhausted all of the possibilities with your current employer (different job, different boss, different arrangement with the current boss, different department, and so on). It is always a good idea to discuss your situation with one or more knowledgeable and objective people not employed in your organization before making a decision to look elsewhere.

If you are looking for a new position with your current employer, you almost certainly need to talk to your current boss about that. In most organizations, the fact that you are seeking a change will get back to your boss very quickly, so it is usually better to tell them at the outset, and get their support, if possible.

YOUR BOSS IS A KEY FIGURE

Whether you're looking for a new job inside or outside your current organization, your current boss is a key figure. That person is likely to be contacted as a reference, whether you list them or not. With an inside change, your boss probably has the power to make it easier or more difficult. So in the end, it's good if you and your boss have a friendly relationship. If you do not, it's a good idea to do whatever you can to create one before starting to look for a new job.

When actually conducting a search while employed, you need to be more cautious, since some techniques can notify your current employer of your intentions. Recruiters are generally safer, as are advertised positions if you're sure they are not your current employer. The central problem is that a good job search demands that you talk to a lot of people—but the more people you talk to, the more likely it is that your current employer will learn of your intentions.

USING THE PIERSON METHOD

The Pierson Method is summarized in the chart below. You may want to use this as a checklist and reference as you work on your search.

Not everyone does these 12 steps in the order listed. For example, you might discover early on that employment agencies or recruiters are likely to work for you and so you'll move to Step 8 quickly—soon after writing a resumé. Or you might prefer to prepare for interviewing and salary negotiations earlier, even before you get a search started. If it does not delay the start of your search, it can be a good idea, since you never know when you'll get your first interview.

I don't care if you follow all 12 steps of the Pierson Method or not. What I'm most concerned about is that you find a good new job, work that you like, and that you'll do well in. And that it doesn't take you too long to do that.

So it's okay with me if you find that great new job when you've only done one or two of the steps, or before you finish your resumé, or even before you finish reading this book. And it's okay with me if you never learn the Pierson Method, or if you forget the whole thing because you're busy working in your new job.

GET READY:
PLAN AND PREPARE
1. Read The Pierson Method book
2. Create a Project Plan and Target List
3. Do a Reality Check on your Project Plan
4. Write your resumé

GET MOVING:
TAKE A SYSTEMATIC APPROACH
5. Gather information on your targets
6. Talk to insiders, Decision Makers, and everyone else
7. Follow up regularly
8. Test the Seven Search Techniques

MANAGE YOUR SEARCH:
USE PROGRESS MEASUREMENTS
9. Track your progress each week
10. Check your Project Plan regularly
11. Interview
12. Start your new job and do well in it

But if you haven't found a job yet, keep using the Pierson Method. If you're not always using all of it, keep doing it the best you can. Even if you feel like you're just stumbling through it, stay with the system. Keep talking to people. Be as organized and positive as you can. And don't give up. Don't quit.

You will succeed.

May your next job be a really good one. May you find it soon.

ORVILLE'S JOURNAL

WE DISCUSS JESSIE'S SEARCH, BUT NOT VERY MUCH, SINCE THIS IS A CELEBRATION

Jessie, Ben, my wife Judy, and I were seated at a round table in a luxurious Chinese restaurant. The waiters bring course after course and put them on a lazy Susan in the middle of the table. The patrons turn it, sampling one delicacy after another.

"Here's to Jessie," Judy said, raising her wine glass. "May you be happy and successful in your new job. And may you have a great teaching career one day."

"Yes," I said. "Congratulations on a well-managed search and a great new job."

"Hear, hear," added Ben.

"Thank you, thank you," replied Jessie, smiling broadly. "I couldn't have done it without the three of you. And that's a fact."

"Jessie," I said, "since Ben and I are your Job Search Work Team and Judy is an honorary team member, I think you need to round out the program by giving us the Final Report on your search."

"All right. Let me see if I remember what I'm supposed to tell you. I talked to 11 different Decision Makers—about half the normal number, so I guess I was lucky on that one."

"Or talented," said Ben, "and a hardworking job hunter."

"I had about 150 job search conversations, but it wasn't 150 different people, since I talked to some people again and again. What else am I supposed to say?"

I ticked off the items. "I know you made about half a dozen staffing firm contacts and got no interviews. How many ads? How many insider contacts, especially peers?"

Jessie gave us the list. "I answered about 60 ads altogether. I got two callbacks. One was a company that was very interested, but they're 100 miles from here. Way too far to commute. The other one went nowhere. I had about a dozen insiders, mostly peers. Should I have brought my records?"

"No," said Judy. "This is a party. Orville sometimes forgets things like that. He's all about job hunting."

"You're right," I said. "That's what I do. But can I ask Jessie one more thing? It's much more interesting than the numbers."

"Sure," said Judy, "but after that, we get on with the celebration."

"It's a deal," I said. "Jessie, please tell us the story of how your search went. Break it into chapters and give each chapter a title."

"Hey, wait a minute," Ben said. "You told Judy it was one more thing. But now you're asking her to write a novel. This could take until midnight. I'm hungry."

"It's okay," said Jessie, "I remember reading this one in Orville's book. It'll only take a minute. It's four chapters. The first chapter was 'Before the Pierson Method.' Nothing was working. I was in a bad mood all the time. And to tell the truth, I wasn't really doing much either. I pretty much wasted three months."

"I'm glad that chapter is over," Ben put in.

"Chapter 2," said Jessie, "is titled, 'A State of Shock.' It started when Orville's book said I'd have to talk to 25 Decision Makers. 'Wow!' I thought. 'This guy's nuts. I'll never talk to that many. It's just not possible.'

"But then I calmed down. I got started with Chapter 3 of my search, which I'll call 'Let's get to it.' I saw that my search was disorganized. It wasn't working. So I decided to get serious about the Pierson Method."

"The part I liked best," Ben added, "was the part where you calmed down."

"Well, it's not like I stayed calm all the time," Jessie said. "I had my ups and downs. Especially when I thought I had the Western job and it didn't happen. The fourth and last chapter I'm going to call, 'Making Some Hits,' because I realized that interviews and offers aren't the only things that count. Talking to the right people counts too. So the insiders I talked to were real 'hits' for me. And talking with friends who turned out to know all kinds of things. Including you, Judy. Thanks."

"You're welcome," Judy said. She's very polite, my wife. And cute too.

Jessie continued, "And one of those hits was the interview for the job I got. It just came out of the blue. The Decision Maker called and invited me in for an interview."

I waved my hands to interrupt. "Wait. Hold on. It wasn't out of the blue. You talked to two insiders over there. You actually said hello to the Decision Maker once. That's not out of the blue. That's the Pierson Method."

"Yes, I suppose it is." Jessie smiled. "But we're not talking job hunting anymore. That's the end of my story. And the official end of my search. Now we're going to eat. Ben looks hungry. And Orville hasn't eaten anything but cookies for weeks."

"Which is completely normal for him," Judy said.

We laughed and turned the lazy Susan. It had filled to overflowing while Jessie was telling her story. We served up some great food, and the celebration began.

The Job Search Work Team (JSWT)

An advisory panel

A core network

A task support group

A project management team

Designed to help people find better jobs faster.
This special section tells you how to start one.

Team Up for a Successful Search: Leading Job Search Work Teams

This special section covers Job Search Work Teams, a great addition to the Pierson Method of job search. You don't need to read it to learn how to find a job. But if you'd like to work with others while you're in search, this section will show you how. And if you want to set up a program to help a lot of people find jobs, this section is definitely for you. These teams are very well suited for use in churches, synagogues, and community organizations. More information on this use can be found at www.highlyeffectivejobsearch.com.

I first discovered Dr. Nathan Azrin's Job Clubs when I was managing services in a career center for unemployed steelworkers in 1983. I had talked to many professionals in job search assistance who used the term Job Club, but they had very different ideas about what it was. So I went back to Azrin's original formula.

The original Job Clubs were proven to reduce time to placement and increase compensation. In studies sponsored by the U.S. Department of Labor, 80 percent of Job Club graduates found new employment within the limits of the pilot versus 46 percent of the control group. Time to placement for Job Club members was less than one-third the time required for control group members. Salaries of Club members were one-third higher. But the Azrin Job Clubs were designed only for people at the lowest income levels.

I liked job clubs because they had people helping each other, seeing job search as a work project, and perhaps even enjoying it. Most important, I liked it because it solved some central problems in job search. People looking for new jobs, as you saw in Chapter 3, often do not do very much useful work each week. As an antidote to this problem, Azrin used some simple progress measurements. I created the Progress Chart in Chapter 11 for the same reasons.

In the early 1990s I redesigned the Job Club as a team for people of any employment level. When I joined a major career services company, Lee Hecht Harrison (LHH), in 1992, the company was looking for better ways to help unemployed people find jobs. The LHH Job Search Work Teams have proven very effective for many thousands of people around the world. Now I am happy to be able to offer you a special do-it-yourself version of JSWT created especially for use by ordinary job hunters with no training in career consulting.

Most of this chapter describes the standard JSWT (as we will abbreviate it), designed for groups of 12 unemployed people. At the end of this chapter you'll find three alternate versions, designed to make it easier for one person to get team support for a single job search, in smaller or virtual teams. These variations of JSWT use many of the features of the standard version and are effective for employed as well as unemployed people.

WHAT JOB SEARCH WORK TEAMS DO

The purpose of the team is simple: the appropriate placement of each team member as soon as possible. The team functions as:

- An advisory panel that provides guidance in dealing with day-to-day issues and problems of job hunting. By hearing—and providing—advice on a wide range of practical issues, team members learn more quickly how to conduct an effective search.

- A core network that expands your personal network by sharing leads, information, and contacts. Team meetings are designed to accelerate networking within the group, and the team becomes a learning laboratory for networking.

- A task support group that encourages members to support each other in their search projects. Team members pledge a limited amount of time each week to assist other members. The team is a supportive community of people in transition.

- A project management team that helps you monitor your progress, providing support to keep your search focused and productive.

How the Job Search Work Team Can Help You

It keeps your search moving.
It keeps you focused and on the right track.
You get objective advice.
It makes a tough job more pleasant.

The single most important factor affecting how long a job search takes is how hard—and how consistently—you work on it. As you saw in Chapter 3, there are numerous barriers to productivity in job search. One reason for creating Job Search Work Teams was to help people overcome those barriers. JSWT graduates often say that a major team benefit was that "it kept me moving."

The Progress Chart in Chapter 11 is very useful in your search—and even more useful when you can talk to other people who are also using it. That chart, your Project Plan, and your Target List are all tools used in Job Search Work Teams to help keep everyone focused and on the right track.

THE TEAM PROVIDES OBJECTIVE ADVICE

The team also serves as a sounding board—a place where you can get objective opinions from other people who understand search. This is important since it is all too easy to take things personally or lose sight of the fact that the Decision Maker and the organization may not see things the same way you do. In search, as in other situations in life, sometimes people who are not directly involved can see situations more clearly and suggest new and better approaches.

YOU ARE NOT ALONE

Perhaps most important is the fact that job search can be a lonely, discouraging activity. You may need to persist in spite of the barriers we discussed in Chapter 3. Getting together with other people to discuss—and maybe even laugh about—job search makes the job of finding a job more pleasant.

TYPES OF TEAMS

There are four types of Job Search Work Teams. Most of this chapter describes the standard JSWT. The other three are variations of the standard version: virtual, one person, and teams for employed people. You need to understand the standard version before reading about the variations, described below and discussed in detail on pages 262–265.

STANDARD JSWT: ONGOING, FOR UNEMPLOYED ONLY

The standard version involves up to 12 unemployed members getting together in person for a two-hour meeting once a week. As people find jobs and leave the team, they are replaced by new members.

Mixing employed and unemployed in this group is not a good idea, since their needs and the pace of their searches can be very different. This version is the one most suitable for not-for-profit organizations that want to provide job search assistance for their members.

VIRTUAL JSWT: LIKE STANDARD, BUT DONE BY PHONE AND E-MAIL

If you are unemployed and not a member of a group offering JSWT, you can assemble one yourself by locating friends and acquaintances looking for jobs. You can also get a group together by using Internet message boards or discussion groups. Naturally, you will want to choose your members carefully, and all members should be familiar with the Pierson Method.

The virtual team meets by telephone conference call (you can also use three-way calling) for 90 minutes each week, with members talking to each other by e-mail and phone between meetings. Membership should be four to seven people at any one time, replacing departing members with new ones. You can find more information on virtual teams on page 262.

JSWT FOR ONE PERSON: EASIER TO GET STARTED

If you are unemployed and not inclined to set up a team with other unemployed people, you can set up a "private" team for just you. This is the kind of team that Jessie, Orville, and Ben set up in Chapter 11. You will need the help of one to three other people who are not looking for new employment and who are willing to help you. Your meetings are either weekly or twice a month, lasting 45 minutes at the most, and can be virtual or in person. You are the only "active" participant—the others are there to assist you. You can find more information on JSWT for one on page 263.

JSWT FOR EMPLOYED PEOPLE: LESS FREQUENT MEETINGS

Teams for employed people typically meet twice a month, on the first and third Monday, for example. They put primary emphasis on career advancement inside of the current employer, looking outside only if all possibilities inside have been exhausted. Because members are employed and have less time for search, they move more slowly. They can be standard or virtual. You can find more information on JSWT for employed people on page 264.

The Standard Job Search Work Team Meeting

A two-hour weekly meeting, including:
Progress Reports (30 minutes)
Advisory panel discussion (90 minutes)
Optional discussions after the meeting (30 to 60 minutes)

Standard JSWT meetings are scheduled for two hours each week. It's best to always have them at the same time and in the same place. The meeting should start promptly at the scheduled time and end at the scheduled time or earlier. This structure is important, since it supports people in better structuring their job searches. An effective meeting helps everyone become more effective in job search.

Team meetings should take place in an informal setting, with participants and the leader sitting in a circle or around a table, never in a classroom arrangement. The team is best led by a leader who is not in search, though rotating the leadership among members is also possible. The materials required are an easel and flipchart (or chalkboard or whiteboard) and a Pierson Method Wall Chart, which appears at the end of this chapter and can be downloaded from the highlyeffectivejobsearch.com site.

The structure of a JSWT meeting is simple, consisting of two activities:

Progress Reports (about 30 minutes). Members briefly report on their progress during the past week and their priorities for the coming week. Members may also suggest agenda topics related to issues or problems they have encountered in their search that are appropriate for advisory panel discussion. Reports always follow the format described below. They are kept to three minutes or less per person, using a timer.

Advisory Panel Discussion (about 90 minutes). The main part of the meeting is a group discussion of general interest job search topics, the agenda items suggested by members in their reports. All team members function as an advisory panel, assisting with these agenda items. This is explained on page 250.

OPTIONAL POSTMEETING DISCUSSIONS

The meeting room should be available for an additional 30 to 60 minutes after the meeting for those who wish to further discuss issues that were raised or to otherwise help each other. This is an opportunity for committees (see page 259) to get their work done and for members to informally exchange information. It may also be an opportunity for socializing.

JSWT Progress Reports

Three minutes per person, including:

1. **Your numbers: From your Progress Chart.**
2. **Your highlights: What worked best last week.**
3. **Your priorities: For the coming week.**
4. **Agenda items: Search issues you want to discuss.**

The first part of a team meeting consists of each team member giving a three-minute Progress Report. It is important that this reporting take no more than about 30 minutes for the entire team, or three minutes per person. That way, plenty of time is left for the advisory panel discussion, which is the heart of the meeting. The easiest way to control this is to have an appointed timekeeper with a stopwatch or kitchen timer.

Team members need to learn how to give totally positive three-minute reports that cover the four areas listed below, without rambling or digressing. This takes a bit of practice. Planning the report before the meeting and making notes on what you will say is always a good idea. Let's look at what's included in each part of the report.

1. NUMBERS: HOW MUCH WORK DID YOU DO LAST WEEK?

In the first part of your Progress Report, you simply read the numbers from your Pierson Method Progress Chart (see Chapter 11) for the last week in search. This takes only 15 to 30 seconds. As members give their reports, the leader writes the numbers on a Pierson Method Wall Chart posted in front of the room. These charts are available from the Web site www.highlyeffectivejobsearch.com.

2. HIGHLIGHTS: WHAT WORKED BEST LAST WEEK?

The next item in your report is a listing of the highlights of your week in search. This normally takes one to two minutes. The highlights should outline the three most useful events—those that resulted in the most progress. They may include:

- A small step in the right direction
- A major breakthrough
- An achievement—something that made your search move a little faster
- A "gift from God"—something that was useful even though it seemed you did nothing to make it happen
- A search problem solved or a difficulty overcome

Highlights are by definition 100 percent positive. If anyone wants to tell a negative story or talk about a problem, they should be asked to convert it into an agenda item so the team can help solve it. Members who say they have no highlights should be prompted by the leader to reconsider the week's activities and events. The definition of highlights is "the three best things that you did or that happened," so anyone who spent time in a search has some.

Highlights are often stories about search. In order to complete your report in three minutes, it is important NOT to tell the entire story, but just to tell the team its title or a very brief outline of it. Members who want to hear the whole story should ask after the meeting.

An example is: "My first highlight is the conversation I had with my sister. She gave me three introductions, including one to an insider—a peer contact at my number four target company. Second, I answered five ads this week, the most I've ever seen in one week. And third, I added six good new organizations to my Target List, two from Internet research, and four from talking to people."

3. PRIORITIES: WHAT YOU WILL DO NEXT WEEK?

The third item in the Progress Report is mentioning the first two or three items on your to-do list for your next week in job search. This should take about 30 seconds. Again, do NOT tell all the details, just name the items.

You should select your priorities for the week by referring to your Project Plan and Target List. Priority to-do's are usually about which organizations you will pursue, what research you will do, and which people you plan to talk to. By mentioning targets by name, you also remind the team to look for information for you.

For example, you might say, "This week I'm concentrating on consulting companies that provide computer-related training for businesses and not-for-profits. I'll be looking for insiders to tell me how these firms work—what they charge, what courses they offer, what they pay employees, and anything else I can find out. My top three targets in this area right now are CompTrain, Delta Training, and PC Education Associates."

If any members had useful information, they would simply say, "I've got something for you. Talk to me after the meeting," rather than taking the team's time to pass the information on during the reports.

4. AGENDA ITEMS: WHAT DO YOU WANT TO DISCUSS WITH THE TEAM IN THIS MEETING?

In this part of the report, lasting perhaps 30 seconds, you may suggest a search-related agenda item for discussion later in the advisory panel portion of the meeting. These optional agenda items are always about how to make your search a little (or a lot) more effective this next week than it was last week. They are therefore of general interest to the entire team, since everyone wants a more effective search. Items of interest to only one person only—such as completing your Project Plan, resumé, or Professional Objective—are handled in committees, not in the team meeting. (See page 258 for examples of agenda items.)

This section of the report is not a place for complaining about difficulties in search or about the state of the job market. Pointing to a difficulty in the job market, for example, is useful only if you make it an agenda item and find a way to overcome that difficulty.

As agenda items are mentioned, the team leader assists the individual in making a concise statement of the agenda item, always stating it in the form of a question. When the member agrees that it is correctly stated, the leader records the item on a flipchart, whiteboard, or chalkboard, with the member's name next to the item. Agenda items should not be discussed as they come up but simply noted for discussion during the advisory panel portion of the meeting.

The JSWT Advisory Panel Discussion

The team leader prioritizes agenda items.
Members discuss the agenda items brought up in the reports.
The leader facilitates the advisory panel discussion.

After about 30 minutes of reporting, the remaining 90 minutes are used for an advisory panel discussion of the agenda items offered by members as part of their reports.

The first step in this part of the meeting is checking and prioritizing the agenda items that have been listed. All items must be about job search, not about personal problems, even if those are barriers to success in search. The leader should try to connect anyone with a personal problem with an appropriate resource for assistance after the meeting. If any search-related items that apply only to one person have been listed, they should be referred to the most appropriate committee.

Normally, there are about half the number of agenda items as there are people in attendance. In a meeting of 10, you would expect five agenda items to be listed. If there are fewer, members should be given another chance to add some.

To prioritize the items, the leader asks for a show of hands. Members vote for the three items they think they would personally benefit most from. The leader records the vote next to the item and numbers the items, from the highest to the lowest vote numbers. Then the leader assigns a length of time to each, generally giving more discussion time to items higher on the list. The times should add up to 10 minutes less than the remaining time in the meeting. All items are discussed, no matter how many votes they got.

After the items are prioritized and a maximum discussion time is assigned to each, the leader facilitates a discussion of each item. The timekeeper ensures that each discussion stays inside its assigned time limit. If the leader and the member who proposed the item agree that the discussion was successful before the allotted time is used, the discussion ends then. At the end of each discussion, the leader summarizes the main points that were made.

The JSWT Contract

Members agree to:
1. **Attend and report**
2. **Respect**
3. **"Doughnuts and Debriefing"**
4. **Two to four hours**

JSWT members sign a contract with the team, promising to do four things that have proven essential to making the team work. The entire contract can be found in the Additional Resources section of this book, and an 8½- by 11-inch copy can be downloaded from the Web site www.highlyeffectivejobsearch.com. The contract includes the following items:

1. ATTEND EVERY MEETING POSSIBLE AND PROVIDE A REPORT EVEN WHEN YOU DO NOT

The reason for regular attendance is simple. Each member of the team serves as a resource and advisor to the other members. If attendance is low, there are fewer resources in the room. Fewer resources means fewer opportunities to receive and give advice, to share networking experiences, and to educate and support one another. This agreement to attend whenever possible helps build a strong, committed community.

You are expected to send your usual Progress Report to the team with another member if you need to miss a meeting. It should include your numbers, highlights, and priorities—but not agenda items, since you won't be there to discuss them.

The information in your report is essential to the team helping you with your search. This commitment to report when not attending also diminishes the temptation to skip meetings on a week when the Progress Report is not as good as usual (which is exactly the week when attending is most important).

Any member who does not attend and does not submit a report through another member should be telephoned immediately after the meeting by the team leader or an assigned member. The caller should inquire about the problem that prevented honoring the promise to send in a report, and then get a commitment that two reports will be submitted next week.

2. TREAT FELLOW TEAM MEMBERS WITH RESPECT

This agreement could be summarized as, "Do unto others as you would have them do unto you." It helps create a caring and supportive community. It also specifically requires that you resign from the team in person, at a meeting, if you decide to leave it before you have found new employment.

3. MAKE A FINAL REPORT TO THE TEAM WHEN YOU FIND A NEW JOB—AND PROVIDE REFRESHMENTS TO CELEBRATE ("DOUGHNUTS AND DEBRIEFING")

This commitment requires you to make a final "debriefing" report—and bring the team doughnuts or other refreshments—when you accept a new job. The debriefing is a very useful learning device for the team. There is a copy of the Final Report to the team at the end of this chapter, and it can also be downloaded from www.highlyeffectivejobsearch.com.

This Final Report is given in the first 15 minutes (or less) of a team meeting, before the Progress Reports. It is timed to ensure that it does not run longer, since there are still unemployed members needing assistance. After the debriefing, the individual may leave the room or stay and participate one last time. Teams often choose to continue the celebration of the success after the meeting.

4. DONATE TWO TO FOUR HOURS TO OTHER TEAM MEMBERS EACH WEEK

Observing the maximum time is just as important as observing the minimum, since your primary duty is to find yourself a new job.

This is most commonly done by participating in or chairing one of the team's committees. Another possibility is working with a new member to help them get started on the team, or working with someone one-to-one on some facet of their search that you are good at. Resumé writing, letter writing, interview practice, and Internet research are all typical committee and one-to-one topics.

Most teams do not formally track this time. Arrangements for its use are facilitated by the leader during the meeting or immediately afterward. Members also make their own arrangements to meet with each other and get the work done.

Eight Things Team Members Do

1. Read *The Unwritten Rules of the Highly Effective Job Search*.

2. Draft a Project Plan.

Read this book—and at least one other book.

One of the reasons the team works is that everyone is using the same job search system, the Pierson Method, so it is important that everyone has read this book. Also, by reading this special section on teams, future members learn how the JSWT works.

In addition to reading this book, everyone should read at least one other book on careers or job search. The team works best when different members read different second books. This outside reading makes advisory panel discussions richer, because each member is not only bringing in their own life experience, but also a wide range of specific job search expertise from their reading. Books are suggested on the highlyeffectivejobsearch.com site.

This reading accelerates the creation of a community body of wisdom on search. It also ensures that new people do not repeatedly ask the same basic questions in team meetings.

DRAFT A PROJECT PLAN

Members-to-be need to draft a Project Plan before joining the team. The team should make members' time and committee assistance available to newcomers. It is important that each new member has at least a tentative Project Plan in place before joining the team. All team members need to actually be conducting a search—as distinguished from preparing to conduct one—and a drafting Project Plan enables a person to get started. The plan can then be refined as the search gets underway.

Eight Things Team Members Do

3. Visit the team to observe.

4. Get oriented by a "search buddy."

5. **Sign the contract and join the team.**
6. **Prepare reports and agenda items in advance.**

VISIT THE TEAM TO OBSERVE AND GET ORIENTED BY A "SEARCH BUDDY"

Throughout the process, new members learn from the experience of existing members. New members should not give a report or propose any agenda items at their first meeting. They may offer ideas and suggestions, but should be cautious about that until they see how meetings work.

During the meeting, the leader helps locate an existing member who is willing to volunteer to assist the new member in getting oriented and getting started. This more experienced "search buddy" works with the new person for the first three weeks, assisting them in preparing their report and possible agenda items, going over the contract with them and orienting them as to how the team works.

SIGN THE CONTRACT AND JOIN THE TEAM

In their second or third meeting—when they and their search buddy think they are ready—new members offer their signed contract to the team. The team accepts by having three team members (not including the leader) also sign it, symbolizing the individual's agreement with the entire group.

PREPARE REPORTS AND AGENDA ITEMS IN ADVANCE

Members should always prepare their reports before the meeting. Immediately before the meeting is usually best, since the report covers the previous seven days. Agenda items should be thought out carefully, and perhaps checked with another member to make sure they meet the criteria for agenda items (see page 250).

Eight Things Team Members Do

7. **Observe Orville's Rules of Order at the meetings.**
8. **Refine the Project Plan while conducting a search.**

OBSERVE ORVILLE'S RULES OF ORDER AT THE MEETINGS

The JSWT is much, much less formal than meetings conducted by Robert's Rules of Order, but some standards are needed, so JSWTs use Orville's Rules of Order, listed below.

REFINE THE PROJECT PLAN WHILE CONDUCTING A SEARCH

It is important for team members to constantly be looking for evidence that their Project Plan is working. After the initial reality checks described in Chapter 9, team members should continue to collect information, especially from target organization insiders, that their search is on the right track. Whenever information suggests a possible weakness in the Project Plan, the member should consult with other team members (outside of the meeting, since this issue is particular to one person) or with the Project Plan Committee.

Orville's Rules of Order

1. **All conversations are constructive.**
2. **Three-minute time limit.**

ALL CONVERSATIONS ARE CONSTRUCTIVE

While there are numerous problems and barriers in job search, complaining about them does not help—it just creates a negative environment. Rather than complaining about a problem in search, you should make an agenda item out of it and solve it. Complaints that have nothing to do with job search are simply a waste of time in a JSWT meeting and are therefore not permitted during the meeting.

This is not to say that people should be unsympathetic to each other's problems. It is simply to say that the team's mission is getting people reemployed, and it's smart to use 100 percent of the two hour team meeting to positively focus on that. Members can and do assist each other with other concerns outside of the meeting.

Advisory panel members need to be especially careful not to criticize the person who proposed the agenda item. The discussions should all be in a group problem-solving mode, with everyone's full participation, looking for the full range of possible solutions.

THREE-MINUTE TIME LIMIT

Just as the reports are limited to three minutes, other speeches are too. The 90-minute discussion period is enough time for 10 members to speak three different times for three minutes each time.

While it is not necessary for all members to have equal "air time" in the meeting, it is important that no one—not even the leader—monopolize the meeting. With 10 people in the meeting, 15 minutes is the most anyone should be talking. This is a rule of thumb, not a hard and fast rule.

People's speeches should NOT be routinely timed. If someone seems to be talking more than is useful, it is the leader's job to speak with them privately, outside of the meeting, about their use of time and this rule. If you are concerned about another member's behavior, you should speak to the person privately. It is very important that no one be publicly criticized during a team meeting.

Orville's Rules of Order

3. Agenda items are for everyone.

Agenda items discussed in the team meeting should always concern the "how to's" of job search, the methods and techniques used by everyone. They are therefore helpful to all members, since everyone in search sooner or later faces the same issues and situations.

Many concerns that initially seem personal, such as, "How can I get an appointment with Mr. Smith," can be generalized into something that helps everyone, such as, "What is the best way to get an appointment with a Decision Maker?"

Some concerns, particularly those about your personal Project Plan or resumé, are very difficult to generalize. These should be handled outside of the team meeting, rather than as agenda items.

Orville's Rules of Order

4. Agenda items must be actionable.

5. Suggestions are for everyone.

AGENDA ITEMS MUST BE ACTIONABLE

In order to be useful to all members, agenda items need to have immediate practical application. General, theoretical items like "What is networking?" are not very useful. Your agenda items should always be about how you can do better in your search next week than you did last week. When the team is discussing your item, you should be listening for the one or two things you can actually do in the next few days. The best way to formulate an agenda item is to ask yourself:

"In the last seven days of my search, what did not go as well as I wish it had?"

"Which part of my plan for next week am I unsure about how to accomplish?"

Focus on one of those and ask a question that will help you improve. Some examples are:

"When I have an appointment to visit an insider at a target organization, what are the best questions to ask?"

"How can I get more referrals from general network contacts?"

"How often should I follow up with a Decision Maker, and what is the best way?"

"What should I do after an interview when they don't call me as they promised to do?"

SUGGESTIONS ARE FOR EVERYONE

When discussing an agenda item, you should not address your suggestions only to the person who asked the question. You should offer your suggestions to the entire group. This way, in addition to helping the person who posted the item, you also help others who will later face the same issue. It also avoids putting too much focus on one person and what they are doing—which can lead to criticizing their activities and undermine group support.

Standing Committees
Project Plan and resumé
Job market research and Internet
Communications practice
Interviewing and negotiations

There are four typical standing committees. Each is composed of and chaired by team members, using their two to four hours per week. Each has a chairperson and vice chairperson chosen by members in consultation with the JSWT leader. When the chairperson finds new employment, the vice chairperson takes over. Both leadership roles need to always be filled. Sometimes some committees will have only the two chairpersons as members. When team membership is low, committees may need to be combined.

Members and prospective members bring their needs to the committee chairperson, who finds the best way to meet those needs. It may be having the individual meet with the entire committee, or it may be pairing the member with the right committee member. In each of the many subject areas, the more experienced and knowledgeable members assist the less experienced and less knowledgeable. The committee's role is also to collect resources, which can include books, Web sites, people outside of the JSWT, and local organizations offering needed assistance.

It is very important that no committee member or chairperson spend more than four hours a week assisting others, since their primary job is to find a new job for themselves.

MULTIPLE TEAMS

When more than one team is sponsored by the same organization, the teams can form their committees jointly. In this case, there can be a larger number of committees, so that Project Plan and Resumé could be two separate committees, for example, or there could be a separate Career Planning committee. In any case, committees should be adjusted to best meet the needs of members and use the talents of committee members.

This arrangement also allows members of one team to work with members of other teams, which can be a networking and learning advantage for everyone.

The Team Leader
Facilitating meetings
Contracts and rules

Ideally, the team leader is not in search and has related skills, such as Human Resources, recruiting, job search assistance, career counseling, or outplacement. In addition, the team leader should be:

- Someone who understands careers and job search
- Personally committed to the mission of the team and the success of each member
- A person with good meeting facilitation skills

When a team member is leader, the team should elect the person they believe has the best combination of the above three skills.

Whether the leader is a member or not, there should always be an alternate leader who is a team member. The alternate leader leads the meeting if the regular leader is unavailable. If the team has decided that it will always be led by a member, the alternate leader becomes leader when the leader finds a job. Then a new alternate leader is selected.

The leader's job includes:

- Start and end meetings on time
- Summarize key points at the end of each agenda item discussion
- Make sure everyone gets a chance to participate in discussions
- Screen agenda items to see that they meet the rules
- Help generalize agenda items when necessary
- Prioritize the agenda items
- Remind members to follow Orville's Rules of Order and honor their contracts

The most difficult part of the leader's job is seeing that everyone abides by all of Orville's Rules of Order and the contract agreements. When a member does not, the leader should speak to them privately—not during the meeting—to assist them in better working on the team. A person who repeatedly ignores rules and agreements and does not improve when asked by the leader should be spoken to privately by the alternate leader as well. If this still produces no improvement, they must be asked to leave the team, since failing to do so will damage the team's ability to help its members.

You have just finished reading a description of the standard JSWT and how to use that kind of team to support people in job search. The standard version is most often used by organizations like churches, synagogues, and community groups, since it serves an ongoing stream of unemployed people and its larger teams need a physical place to meet. If you want to start your own team and be the first member of it, the virtual team might be a better choice.

The Virtual Team

Has four to seven members.

Conducts 90-minute meetings by telephone conference call.

Uses a virtual wall chart.

Every member talks to two others.

No committees.

Since members do not need to leave home to attend meetings, the virtual team is more convenient and members can be spread out over a wider area. If you find members on the Internet, you can select people with similar work backgrounds, regardless of where they live. On the other hand, keeping it local can cut phone bills for conference calls or three-way calling. Local groups also have the advantage that members can share knowledge of the local job market, and a diversity of occupational backgrounds also has advantages.

Telephone meetings work better with smaller groups, and four to seven people has proven to be about right for a virtual team, with the maximum meeting length at 90 minutes rather than two hours. Because members cannot all see the same wall chart during the meeting, they need to e-mail their Progress Chart numbers to each other prior to the meeting. Each member should keep their own wall chart for the entire group, writing in the numbers as they are read during the meeting. Members must recite the numbers in their reports out loud, even though they were also e-mailed.

TALK TO EACH OTHER BETWEEN MEETINGS

Virtual JSWT members need to pay special attention to talking to each other between meetings. The best way to make sure this happens is to require that each member, as part of the "two-to-four-hour" agreement, talks to at least two other members during the week—and check it during meetings.

While e-mail conversations are also useful, these real-time conversations help ensure that no one feels discouraged and isolated. Although the team is usually too small to have committees, individuals may be selected to fill similar roles.

Because members of a virtual team cannot see each other during meetings, the leader needs to pay particular attention to inviting everyone into the conversation. While no one is required to speak, it can be helpful to ask members who have not spoken on a given agenda item if they have anything to add.

A Team for One Person

One to three advisors
Reports weekly
45-minute meetings weekly or twice a month

Much of the same process can be used with a single job seeker. If you want team support but no JSWT is available, you can start your own small group. You can select as your advisors one to three people who are committed to your success.

They should not be people with a strong personal connection that could prohibit objectivity—a spouse, parent, or dependent, for example, is usually not a good idea. If you can locate people with some or all of the team leader qualifications, those can be very useful. Someone employed in the field where you plan to be employed can also be a great choice.

This team, which you may want to call an advisory panel, should meet with you for a discussion twice a month, always on the same days (e.g., first and third Tuesday evenings) for a specified time. Forty-five minutes is usually about right. If you and your panel decide twice a month is insufficient, make it weekly. Meetings are similar to the standard team, except that the agenda items are all yours, and you are expected to have at least one at each meeting, and you may have several. Meetings can be virtual or in person.

You are expected to give your weekly Progress Report to all of your panel members every week. On meeting weeks, you can simply bring them to the meeting. On other weeks, you must e-mail, fax, or mail them.

Naturally, all of your panel members must be familiar with the Pierson Method. One panel member should be selected as leader, just as in the standard team. Or this "team" may just be you and one other person. You should use the parts of the contract that are applicable. Naturally, there are no committees and no list of agenda items.

Another variation of the team for one is working with a paid professional career consultant who is familiar with the Pierson Method. If you choose to do this, be sure to read pages 115–116.

JSWT For Employed People

Has meetings twice a month.
Reports twice a month.
Has more latitude on agenda items.
Does not mix employed and unemployed on the same team.

Teams for employed people move more slowly, since employed people have less time to spend on job search. Meetings are therefore scheduled only twice a month. The wall chart is still used, and numbers are posted by week, though each member gives a report covering two or three weeks at each meeting.

The cardinal rule of job search for employed people is to keep their current job until they find a new one, inside or outside of their current employer. They should look outside only if all possibilities inside have been exhausted. And they should do everything possible to create and maintain a positive relationship with their current boss, no matter how poorly that person may behave.

MORE LATITUDE IN TEAM AGENDA ITEMS AND DISCUSSION

Because members may be working on improving their situations at work, conducting an internal search, conducting an external search, or all of these, discussions are more complex. These teams must allow some discussion of personal career issues, so more latitude is given in reporting and in discussions. An individual team member may have up to 15 minutes of discussion time on a personal career issue. No more than four members may do this each week, leaving the remaining time for discussion of issues of general interest.

Smaller teams—of four to seven members, with a two-hour meeting—allow for more time per person. The reporting time remains the same, though members not in search do not report numbers.

RESOURCES FOR TEAM MEETINGS

In the Additional Resources section that follows this chapter, you will find resources for teams of all kinds. Some of these items may also be downloaded in a convenient 8½- by 11-inch format from the highlyeffectivejobsearch.com site.

Summary of the Special Section on Job Search Work Teams

THE JOB SEARCH WORK TEAM MEETING

A two-hour weekly meeting:
Progress Reports (30 minutes)
Advisory Panel Discussion (90 minutes)
Plus optional discussions after the meeting (30 to 60 minutes)

Part One: Progress Reports (30 minutes)
Three minutes per person.
1. Your numbers: How much you accomplished.
2. Your highlights: What worked best last week.
3. Your priorities: For the coming week.
4. Agenda items: Search issues you want to discuss.

Part Two: Advisory Panel Discussion
(90 minutes)
The team leader prioritizes agenda items.
Members discuss the agenda items brought up in the reports.
The leader facilitates the advisory panel discussion.

WHAT IS EXPECTED OF TEAM MEMBERS

The JSWT Contract.

This is what members agree to:
1. Attend and report
2. Respect
3. Doughnuts and Debriefing
4. Two to four hours

Eight Things Team Members Do

1. Read *The Unwritten Rules of the Highly Effective Job Search.*
2. Draft a Project Plan.
3. Visit the team to observe.
4. Get oriented by a "search buddy."
5. Sign the contract and join the team.
6. Prepare reports and agenda items in advance.
7. Observe Orville's Rules of Order at the meetings.
8. Refine the Project Plan while conducting a search.

**What Team Members Do in the Meeting
(Orville's Rules of Order):**

1. All conversations are constructive.
2. Three-minute time limit.
3. Agenda items are for everyone.
4. Agenda items must be actionable.
5. Suggestions are for everyone.

HOW TEAMS ARE ORGANIZED

Standing Committees
(each with a chairperson and vice chairperson)
  Project Plan and Resumé
  Job Market Research and Internet
  Communications Practice
  Interviewing and Negotiations

Team Leader
  Facilitates meetings
  Contracts and rules

THREE ADDITIONAL KINDS OF TEAMS

The Virtual Team
    Four to seven members
    90-minute meetings by telephone conference call
    Uses a virtual wall chart
    Every member talks to two others
    No committees

A Team for One Person
    One to three advisors
    Reports weekly
    45-minute meetings weekly or twice a month

JSWT for Employed People
    Meetings twice a month
    Reports twice a month
    More latitude on agenda items
    Do not mix employed and unemployed
        on the same team

ADDITIONAL RESOURCES

Downloadable 8½- by 11-inch copies of the following forms can be found at highlyeffectivejobsearch.com.

Progress Chart	PAGE 1 (OR FRONT OF TWO-SIDED SHEET)								
DATE (week of)									
Job Search Education									
Research									
Letters and Admin.									
Network: phone									
Network: In person									
TOTAL HOURS									
Direct mail									
Advertised positions									
Search Firms									
Other Letters									
TOTAL LETTERS									
General network (include search firms)									
Target company Miscellaneous contact									
Target company Peer contact									
Target company Decision Maker/above									
Follow-ups with Decision Maker/above									
TOTAL CONTACTS									

DEFINITIONS OF THE CATEGORIES ON THE CHART

TOTAL HOURS. : The total number of hours you spent on job search this week, including job search education, research, letter writing, administration, and talking to people on the phone and in person, each of which has its own row.

Direct mail. The number of letters or e-mails sent to people with whom you have no contact and who have never heard of you.

Advertised positions. The number of responses to ads or Internet postings that you made.

Search firms. The number of letters you sent to search firms or employment agencies.

Other letters. Other letters or e-mails that you sent out. Example: to set up networking meetings.

TOTAL LETTERS.: The total number of letters written and mailed or e-mailed this week.

General network. The number of conversations with people who are not inside of target organizations. Count conversations with search firms here.

Target company, Miscellaneous contact. This category includes all contacts inside of a target organizations, but below your level.

Target company, Peer Contact. Tracking conversations with people who are more or less at your level inside of a target organization. HR people are usually here.

Target company, Decision Maker/above. The most productive conversations are with Decision Makers and managers above the Decision Maker inside of target organizations. A running total of these is important.

Follow-ups with Decision Makers/above. Count second and succeeding conversations with the same Decision Maker (or above) in this row.

TOTAL JOB SEARCH CONVERSATIONS OR "CONTACTS.": The total number of conversations you have in person or on the phone with anyone about your job search this week.

You can find more information on the Progress Chart in Chapter 9 of *The Unwritten Rules of the Highly Effective Job Search.*

The Pierson Method Wall Chart												
NAME	1	2	3	4	5	6	7	8	9	10	11	12
TOTAL HOURS												
Direct Mail												
Advertised Positions												
Search Firms												
Other Letters												
TOTAL LETTERS												
General Network (include Search Firms)												
Target Company Miscellaneous contact												
Target Company Peer contact												
Target Company Decision Maker/above												
Follow-ups with Decision Maker/above												
TOTAL CONTACTS												

How to Use the Job Search Work Team Wall Chart

1. Make a very large copy of the chart, large enough to be posted on the wall and still read by people sitting around a meeting table. This is usually about three feet high by four feet wide. The boxes in the grid will be rectangular, not square.

2. Write team member's names in the numbered spaces at the top with a Magic Marker.

3. Use one wall chart for each team for each month.

4. At the Job Search Work Team meeting, write each team member's numbers for the week in the column under their name. Use a dash (–) rather than a zero when the person has no number for a particular row.

5. Use a different colored Magic Marker for each week of the month. Record each member's numbers for the first week of the month in the upper left quadrant of the each box. Record the second week (in a different color) in the upper right quadrant, the third week in the lower right, and the fourth week in the lower left, proceeding clockwise around each box. Make the four numbers as large as possible, so they can be read from the table.

   This system of using different colors and different corners of the box each week makes it easy to see at a glance how each team member is conducting their search—where they are strong in search and can help others (e.g., getting in to see Decision Makers) and where they are not so strong and may need some help from the team.

6. For those months with five team meetings, squeeze the fifth number into the center of the box. (Don't worry if it's not too legible, the month is over and the chart will soon be replaced with a new one.)

7. When a member finds a new job, write "NEW JOB," "CONGRATULA-TIONS," or whatever you like in big letters in their column, on top of whatever numbers are there.

8. Put a second identical chart on the wall to use only for an "honor roll" of people who found jobs. When they do, put their names in the numbered space at the top and their TOTAL (for the entire search) number of hours, letters, and contacts. This lets other team members see the totals required by various people to find a job.

Name (print) _____

Team name _____

Date _____

One of your commitments to your team is to debrief the team on your entire career advancement project when you finish it. This debriefing is of great importance to the team because it enables your teammates to better understand their own search projects.

Your thoughtful debriefing will help others succeed more quickly, as well as consolidating what you learn from of the project for your own future reference. In giving the report verbally, please use this outline as the basis for a 10- to 15-minute presentation to the team. If you need to start new employment immediately or are otherwise unable to give the report in person, please transmit it through a teammate or in writing in the same format. Please include:

1 Description. A brief description of your new position and organization or details of other career advancement. Mention the two or three things about the job or the organization that were most important in your decision to take it—what you like best about them.

2. Overall Progress Summary. Please calculate the grand totals from your Progress Chart using the chart on the other side of this sheet. Post these on a separate wall chart, reserved for this purpose.

3. The Story of Your Search. Briefly (in about five minutes) tell the story of your entire job search project. In doing so, divide it into phases or chapters, each with a descriptive title. In giving your report, name each of the chapters and give a very brief description of what happened in each. Again, this is an excellent learning experience for your teammates, since some who have successfully completed the project usually have a new perspective on it.

4. Strategy. As your project proceeded, did you modify your Project Plan (i.e., your Professional Objective, your Core Message, or your Target Market criteria)? If so, when and why?

5. Success Factors. What were the most important factors in your success? How did the team (or individual teammates) help you succeed?

6. Advice. Now that you have successfully completed your job search, what advice would you give to your teammates who are still working on their projects? Please keep this to one sentence.

Final Report to the Team PAGE 2 (OR BACK OF TWO-SIDED SHEET)

Category	Average per week	Total for search
TOTAL HOURS		
Direct Mail		
Advertised Positions		
Search Firms		
Other Letters		
TOTAL LETTERS		
General Network (include Search Firms)		
Target Company Miscellaneous contact		
Target Company Peer contact		
Target Company Decision Maker/above		
Follow-ups with Decision Maker/above		
TOTAL CONTACTS		

The Job Search Work Team Contract

As a member of the _____ Job Search Work Team
(name of team)

at _____ **I agree to:**
(name of sponsoring organization)

1. Attend every meeting possible and provide a report even when I do not.

I understand that my regular attendance is important to the team as well as to my job search, so

> **I agree to attend each and every weekly meeting of my JSWT,** scheduling search and personal activities around the JSWT meeting time. I understand that a critical search activity (such as an interview that cannot be scheduled at any other time) or an illness or family emergency are exceptions.

I understand that the team needs to have information on my search in order to help me, so

> **I agree to submit a weekly progress report to the team each week for the duration of my search.** If I am unable to attend a meeting, I will give my weekly progress report (the first three items only) to another team member (not the team leader), who will read it to the team for me and see that my numbers are posted on the Job Search Productivity Wall Chart.

2. Treat team members with respect.

I understand that it is up to each and every member to make the team a pleasant and effective group, so

> **I agree to honor commitments.** I will arrive on time or early for meetings, fulfill my promises to others, follow all rules of the team, and work to ensure that each meeting is productive for all team members, including myself.

> **I agree to resign from the team in person if I decide to leave it before finding a new job.** I understand that unexpected disappear-

ances of team members are disturbing to the team and that integrity and good manners both require my departing in a way that brings closure for all team members.

I agree to support fellow team members in whatever ways I can. This includes offering honest opinions and feedback to fellow team members about their plans and strategies in a positive and caring manner.

I agree to generally treat others as I would like to be treated.

3. Make a Final Report to the team when I find a new job—and provide refreshments (doughnuts or some other treat) for the team at the first meeting after I accept the job.

I understand that celebrating success and understanding the pathways to getting there is important to the team, so

> **I agree to use the standard Final Report form to provide the team with a debriefing of my search.** I will summarize my progress statistics for my entire search, describe the major phases or chapters of my search, tell what I saw as most useful and productive in the course of the search and where the team was most helpful. If I am unable to attend the first team meeting after I find a new job, I agree to provide a written report to another member to read for me.

> **I agree to provide doughnuts** or other appropriate treats for the entire team on the day the Final Report is scheduled, whether I am able to attend that meeting or not.

4. Donate two to four hours to other team members outside of the weekly meeting.

I understand the team works because members help each other get the work done, so

> **I agree to donate a minimum of two hours and a maximum of four hours each week to assisting other team members.** I understand that observing the maximum is just as important as observing the minimum, since my primary duty is to find myself a new job. Specifically, I will look for opportunities to:

Participate in one of the team's committees

Chair one of the team's committees

Work with a new member to help them get started on the team

Work with other members one-to-one on some facet of their search that I am good at—for example, resumé writing, letter writing, interview practice, Internet research. or any other search related work

I understand that this agreement does not require me to do anything that I am uncomfortable with or anything that causes me or my family undue hardship.

I will also do whatever I reasonably can to be a resource to the team or individual team members for six months after I am reemployed, making an effort to donate a total of 10 hours during those six months. To the degree that it is practical and realistic, I will share my contact lists and Target Company information with one or more team members when I have a new job.

5. Abide by the rules.

I agree to abide by all of the other rules of the team as outlined in *The Unwritten Rules of the Highly Successful Job Search*, and I agree to abide by the rules of the organization sponsoring the JSWT program. I understand that my failure to live up to my agreements in this contract can result in the leader asking me to leave the team.

Signed _____ date: _____

(new team member)

Signed _____ date: _____

(experienced team member)

Signed _____ date: _____

(experienced team member)

Signed _____ date: _____

(experienced team member)

What Is Expected of Team Members
REMINDER CARD FOR MEMBERS

The Eight Things Team Members Do

1. Read *The Unwritten Rules of the Highly Effective Job Search.*
2. Draft a Project Plan.
3. Visit the team to observe.
4. Get oriented by a "search buddy."
5. Sign the contract and join the team.
6. Prepare reports and agenda items in advance.
7. Observe Orville's Rules of Order at the meetings.
8. Refine the Project Plan while conducting a search.

What Team Members Do in the Meeting
(Orville's Rules of Order)

1. All conversations are constructive.
2. Three-minute time limit.
3. Agenda items are for everyone.
4. Agenda items must be actionable.
5. Suggestions are for everyone.

ACKNOWLEDGMENTS

This book was made possible by the generosity of Lee Hecht Harrison, LLC (LHH), my current employer. I am grateful to the company for supporting the project and my career, and I am grateful to all the people I have worked with at LHH over the years.

In particular, I would like to thank all of the LHH consultants. On many occasions, I was in the front of the room in the role of trainer, but I learned at least as much from you as you did from me. And I learned even more in the private conversations I had with many of you over the years. It is a great privilege to have such a large group of dedicated career professionals as colleagues and friends.

I hesitated to list any names of LHH staffers, since there are many, many people who made contributions to this book and to my career, and I will surely omit some that should be included. However, I do want to acknowledge some of my colleagues at corporate headquarters without whom this book would not have happened.

First, China Gorman, when she was President and COO, made the arrangements that finally got the project underway, after several previous false starts. Thank you, China. Paul O'Donnell and John Mears, my current boss, have also been very supportive. Ron Braley, Penny Shaw, Winnie Downes, and Bonnie Maitlen were all instrumental in recognizing the value of this material when they agreed to hire me in 1992. I also appreciate the support of others that I reported to: Ray Roe, Bern Kenny, Bob Lee, Doug Marr, and Sharon Bray. My former LHH colleagues and career coaches, Peter Prichard and Anne Raftery, were very supportive from the beginning. Thanks to Rena Lewis for her help with marketing, graphics, and everything else. Three people not on the corporate staff also made very specific offers of assistance. Thank you, Sharon Winston, June Adkinson, and Leigh Moore.

The three LHHers I've worked most closely with are on the LHH Design Team. Thank you, Richard, for keeping an eye on things, so I could look elsewhere. Thank you, Susan Bassett, for being my creative partner on so many projects. And thank you, Gail Watt, for being such a dedicated, excellent writer and editor. You and I have written a lot of books together, and I've learned a lot from you. This is the first major book I've done without you, team. I hope you like it. And, George Nicholson, thanks for your help and support.

Finally, I want to thank you, Steve Harrison, the second H in LHH, for hiring me in the first place, for giving me the opportunity to create and prove innovative new career programs on a large scale, and for your unflagging support for more than a decade.

I'd like also to thank people who were mentors and supporters in my pre-LHH career. First, Bill and Dick Pilder, the leaders of Mainstream Access, one of the very best smaller career firms on the planet, ever. I learned a lot from both of you and from the great staff you put together. Thanks, all.

Special thanks to Jocelyn Sampson, truly a master trainer.

Thanks to Mike King, Bob Chapman, Bill Broussard, and all the others I worked with at their innovative company. Thank you KCB, for your generosity with employee training. You'll see its influence in this book.

Thanks also to Mary McCaulley at CAPT and Pendleton Waggoner at BHA for their mentoring and assistance with the MBTI, whose influence is also visible in this book.

Thank you, Ron Colvin, for getting me started in the field. And Scot Stewart for helping me get established. And my first career coach, Bill Brittain.

A number of people assisted me in writing this book by reading it and providing ideas and suggestions. Thank you, Bill Thomas, my career consulting partner, Kaveri Fettes, Gene and Maureen Nelson, Krishna Maurer, David and Gita Haddad, and Judy Cohen.

A special thank you to Peter Sugarman, an excellent writer and extraordinary writing coach, who read and reread the manuscript and gave some great advice on improving it, including comments that led to the creation of Ben and Jessie.

The book is in print because of the Jeff Herman Agency (if you want to publish, go read Jeff's book). Deborah Levine Herman, also of the Jeff Herman Agency, gave me some excellent coaching on how to write (go read her book too).

Thanks also to Kate Wendleton of the Five O'Clock Club for her assistance, and to Tom Wilinsky.

And of course, this book is in your hands now because of McGraw-Hill Editorial Director Mary Glenn and Associate Editor Monica Bentley. Thanks to both of you for your assistance and counsel, and to Eileen Lamadore, Seth Morris, Scott Kurtz, and Cindy LaBreacht.

My adult children have both made significant contributions to this book. Thank you, Sarah and Paul, for helping solve problems, for coming up with ideas, and for everything else you've done. I've really enjoyed having the book as a family project.

Thank you to my parents for getting me here and so well educated, too.

I always read acknowledgments of and dedications to authors' spouses with a bit of cynicism. What did they do, anyway? Well, now I understand. This book would never have been written if it weren't for my wife, Judy. Thank you for your support over the years, Beauty, and for your help in the writing of this book. It's living with you and having you for a life partner that's made me who I am, and therefore made the book what it is. Anyone who knew me before I met you would agree that you've had an extraordinarily positive influence on me. It's been a blessing to have you in my life, my dear Ramala.

Finally, I want to acknowledge the great teachers and saints who offer us guidance in everything in life and bring us daily closer to God. And I acknowledge God's grace, active in this book as it is in everything, everywhere, always. Thank you, Lord.